GET CARTER

GET CARTER

The Hamish Carter Story

Phil Taylor

Hodder Moa

National Library of New Zealand Cataloguing-in-Publication Data
Taylor, Phil, 1958-
Get Carter : the Hamish Carter story / Phil Taylor.
ISBN 978-1-86971-099-6
1. Carter, Hamish, 1971- 2. Athletes—New Zealand—
Biography. 3. Triathlon—New Zealand. 4. New Zealand—
Biography. I. Title.
796.4257092—dc 22

A Hodder Moa Book
Published in 2007 by Hachette Livre NZ Ltd
4 Whetu Place, Mairangi Bay
Auckland, New Zealand

Designed and produced by Hachette Livre NZ Ltd
Printed by Everbest Printing Co. Ltd., China

Front cover: Hamish Carter wins gold at the Athens Olympics in 2004. Photosport
Back cover: Carter races in the Port of Tauranga team event in early 2006. Photosport

For those who dare to dream . . .

About the Writer

Phil Taylor has worked as a journalist in England and Australia as well as New Zealand where he has won numerous awards including Journalist of the Year, Feature Writer of the Year, Reporter of the Year, and Sports Reporter of the Year. He was awarded fellowships to Green College, Oxford University, in 1996, and Wolfson College, Cambridge University, in 2001. He represented Canterbury in cycling and New Zealand at a world duathlon championship. He currently works as a senior writer covering current affairs for the *New Zealand Herald* and lives in Auckland with his journalist wife, Joanna, and children Flynn and Billie. His interests include watching 'Get Smart' re-runs with the kids and riding his bike. This is his first book.

Contents

Acknowledgements

There have been hundreds of people over the course of my career who have played a part in this story. From where I started to where I am now comes down to one fundamental thing: success comes from the people you have in your team. I could never have scratched the surface without these people who gave me a big knife and taught me how to use it. Thank you, thank you, thank you . . .

Mum and Dad, Cath, Doug, James, Tom. Marisa, my wonderful wife, and our two little monsters Chop and Nic-a-lee. Manager Roger Mortimer. Coaches Chris Pilone and Mark Bone. Legends Dave Currie, John Walker and Tony Hurt. Rowing coaches Barry Cleal and Bryan Goss. My training hacks, friends and competitors: Greg and Laura Bennett, Ben Bright, Cameron Brown, Alan Bunce, Bevan Docherty, Mark and Jude Elliott, Kris Gemmell, Chubb George, Chris Hill, Lou James, Andrew Johns, Richard Lockhart, Nathan Richmond, Liam Scopes, Gary and Chanel Stuck, Debbie Tanner, Phil Taylor, Sarah Ulmer and Doon, Rick Wells, Simon Whitfield, Jason Windhager.

To my sponsors who have been fantastic supporters and great friends through thick and thin: Sanitarium, Hyundai, McDonald's, Hewlett Packard, Air New Zealand, Nike, Purina, Vodafone, Avanti, Orca, Oakley, Cyco, Tri NZ (supported by SPARC) and finally Xero. Not only was their support vital to my success as an athlete, they showed me the business opportunities available to a top athlete.

To my country, it has been an honour to wear the silver fern.

Hamish Carter
June 2007

DESPAIR IN SYDNEY

The finish couldn't come soon enough. The huge crowd lining the course created a rising wave of sound. When you're going well, it's inspiring; but when you aren't, you want the asphalt to swallow you up. I wasn't going well. In the midst of so many people, I felt alone and helpless. It was as though I was running in my sleep, like being in a car that won't shift into top gear. The run seemed to be taking an age. At last, the road tilted downhill towards Sydney Harbour and the finish. I crossed the line and dropped my head. I was in no mood to meet the questioning looks I saw all around me. I was the world number one triathlete, one of the favourites to win an Olympic gold medal in my sport's debut at the Games and I had just finished 26th. I had failed, utterly. What had happened? Everyone wanted to know — me included.

My wife Marisa appeared at my side. She'd jumped a barrier and somehow evaded the officials. She knew what I was going through and ushered me the short distance to the steps of the Opera House. That was the picture on the front of the *New Zealand Herald* the next day: Marisa and I sitting on those steps. It was an image of absolute dejection. The camera didn't lie. A headline on the accompanying story read: 'Medal hopeful Hamish Carter feels he has let the country down.'

This wasn't how it was supposed to turn out.

Since I was a kid, I'd had a belief that's been central to my life — the idea that I was going to be a world-beater. Bizarre, I know, but there it is. Because I grew up with it, it didn't seem odd to me. As young people do with familiar things, I just accepted that that was how it would be. I would work hard, pay my dues and be rewarded by becoming a world-champion sportsman.

I was in my first year at primary school when John Walker won the 1500 metres at the 1976 Olympic Games. He was the first person to run a mile faster than 3 min 50 sec, and at the Games in Montreal he justified his favouritism in the best way possible, charging to the front with 300 metres remaining and holding off all challengers. I was spellbound by the spectacle as much as the deed; his long hair flowing, his arms raised as he hit the line — and the black singlet. That's what I wanted. Fulfilling that dream became my reason for being. It was who I was. I couldn't explain it, can't explain it now; it was just there within me. It is ridiculous, I know, but I believed, unquestioningly, that my destiny was to be the best. It might have been the world championships, it might have been the Olympic Games, whatever, but I would win.

I ran harriers at school, but it was rowing that I loved. I assumed that I'd row my way to the top, but size, or the lack of it, got in the way. I took up triathlon, the swim-bike-run sport, in 1991. Nine years later, I was in Sydney at the 2000 Olympic Games, as close as New Zealand will come to a home Games. I was 29, an age when I could expect to be at the peak of my physical powers. All my family and many friends had travelled to watch me, all expectant. But no one had greater expectations than I did myself. The world title had eluded me — over the years I'd been fifth, fourth, third, second — but what better way to cap three years as triathlon's top-ranked athlete than by winning the Olympic gold medal. It would consummate everything, justify my existence and make sense of how I lived. That's why 17 September 2000 was the worst day of my life. It was also the most important, but we'll come to that.

Twenty-sixth! I sat with my eyes closed for long minutes. I felt all sorts of emotions, but most of all I was angry. What had I done wrong? Why was I being put through this? I was just angry; angry with the team management, angry with myself. What a fool I was to believe that I was destined to win. How could I assume such a thing when there were 49 other guys out there equally desperate to win? Why shouldn't it be their destiny too? It was good to have Marisa with me, even though we hardly spoke. There are no words for such a time. None of my supporters knew what to say and I didn't know what to tell them.

Jack Ralston, Carter's coach

The hardest thing I ever saw was how distraught he was. There were cameras around him and I saw that Marisa was sitting with him, and so I held back. To see tears; you know he was devastated.

I replayed the race in my mind many times, looking for where I went wrong, why it had happened. My ranking meant that I had first pick of the spots on the starting pontoon and I made a good start. The back of my wetsuit came undone, which meant I had to swim hard to stay on the feet of Englishman Simon Lessing, but I managed it. With four world titles under his belt, he was the man to mark. Lessing, the Aussie Craig Walton and I — all strong cyclists — started the bike leg with a handy gap. I thought we were going to get away but on the second lap we were caught and everything changed. Almost the whole field was back together again and there was always someone taking a chance by attacking off the front. That brought out my controlling attitude and, instead of relaxing, I tried to respond to every move. By the end of the ride, two competitors had a one-minute lead, but the race was still there to be won. The eventual winner, Canadian Simon Whitfield, was in the pack with me. In triathlon, if you're having a bad day you might get through the ride but the first few steps you take tell you if you've got your running legs. That's when I knew for sure that I was in big trouble. At such times, it's irrelevant how determined you are or how supportive the crowd is.

The run was two laps of a five-kilometre circuit. The crowd noise was incredible, an indecipherable roar like a jet engine. I managed to pick the voices of a few friends urging me on. 'C'mon, c'mon, go, go, go,' they called, although I was already steadily leaking territory. I dreaded approaching the same point on the second lap. When you're beaten and battling, the cheers sound like pity: 'C'mon mate, keep going'. But when I ran past again, I didn't hear them at all. I felt like crawling into a corner, curling up and hiding away. I couldn't even run faster to make it end sooner. The run seemed the longest half-hour of my life.

I couldn't bring myself to watch the medal ceremony, not for anything. I saw Whitfield a few days later in the Nike tent and I stared at him as though I hated him. Lovely guy and great athlete — and these days, close friend — that he is, he hadn't won a big race before and the way I looked at it, he'd won *my* race. I was jealous and it seemed so unfair. I'd paid my dues. How could I have had the worst race of my career in the most important race ever? Where had I gone wrong? What made it worse was that I had shot my mouth off in the media, fuelling expectation with talk about how well my training was going. I'd said that I felt 'bulletproof'. I sure didn't now. I imagined this must be how a Wall Street dealer would feel having lost $10 million in an afternoon on a sure-fire call.

Having been destroyed by the very thing you do best is not easy to come to terms with. I don't think Jack, my coach, could understand either. We'd thought that we had it dialled; we'd thought we could do it our way. It took me a very long time, but I came to understand that I didn't lose the race just that day. It was lost well before then. For many reasons, I wasn't ready to win a race like that.

Back home I was labelled a loser, 'a waste of money' according to the head of the Sports Foundation, the organisation that tries to pick medal winners and then helps fund them. That hurt. Did they think that I wasn't desperate to win? They made it sound like I pocketed a fortune of the public's money on false pretences. One of my sponsors dropped me.

I'd looked forward to the Olympics for so long and now it was over, and I was one of its victims. God, how I hated what the Olympics stood for. *Citius, Altius, Fortius* (Faster, Higher, Stronger), chivalry, fellowship among men? To me it represented heartbreak and despair. The public get to see only the happy faces, the flags, the anthems and the victors, but there is a whole other side to it that can be grim and downright depressing. You have to get close to see the broader reality. Three people win a medal. Most of the rest are destroyed. Why is sport so unbalanced? Everyone has worked hard to be there and four years of your life goes down the drain in one race.

I tried to remind myself that I was at the Olympic Games and that that alone was something. I stayed, supported other Kiwis at their events and went out in the evenings, but I was stalked by the fact that I'd blown it. Whatever chance I had in that race, I'd lost in the preceding week. I didn't handle the all-encompassing circus that is the Olympics. They sweep you up, chew you over, and if you can't cope with all that the Games entails, you get spat out.

The 2000 Sydney Olympics brought out the worst in me. I knew that I could do much better, but did I want to? For a long time after, whenever I saw snippets of the Games on television, or saw the Olympic rings, it would trigger a feeling of dread. I didn't want anything to do with the Olympic Games. Why would I want to go back to such a brutal environment? But that was the choice. I could give up on my dream and walk away forever, or I could try again.

LIFE'S A BEACH

Friday night meant fish and chips in the Carter residence and fish and chips meant competition. As the youngest of five kids, I had to be on my toes, ready for action as soon as the beautiful, big newspaper-wrapped parcel hit the table. Building up an appetite was never a problem; I spent my days tooling around the neighbourhood on my pushbike and was always hungry. As soon as the paper was stripped away to reveal the steaming golden pile, everyone would put their fish to one side then dive into the mound of chips. The game plan was to gorge on chips — as many as possible, as fast as possible. The chips were the communal part of the meal, so it didn't pay to be slow off the mark. Once you'd stuffed yourself with potato, you could afford to take a breather and enjoy your fish. There was no risk with the fish. They were sacrosanct, designated items and not fair game to poachers.

I guess big families are competitive by nature. There were four of us Carter boys and as far as clothes went, it was a case of first up, best dressed. Everyone would grab whatever they wanted to wear, so if you had a favourite top or pair of pants, it paid to hide it or you'd have to suffer the frustration of seeing one of your brothers swanning around in it.

The Carter kids arrived in this order: Cathy, Doug, James, Tom and, three years later, me, Hamish Clive Carter. I was supposed to be a girl. Mum was keen on a sister for Cathy and I suspect Cathy was too, although she's never had a problem handling her four little brothers. Mum had already had a busy time with pregnancies and baby-rearing by the time I came along when she was thirty, so I was the last roll of the dice as far as kids went. You could say that I owe my existence to tennis elbow. Mum's always had a lot of energy and never been one to waste time, so when injury stopped her playing tennis she decided she'd use the time to have a baby.

I guess Cath must have been disappointed with another brother but the upside was she got to keep her clothes to herself. Being the youngest, I invariably lived in hand-me-downs. The family lived in Lucerne Road, Remuera, when I was born but I have no memory of that house.

Doug Carter

I remember Mum and Dad bringing Hamish home from the hospital when I was eight. They had a cot set up for him in their room and were very excited. I vividly recall thinking, 'Oh God, another one!' We were already a big family, and here was one more, bringing the tally to one girl and four boys. I wasn't impressed but the truth is that Mum was crazy about kids.

I was raised in a big old house on Mountain Road, opposite Auckland Grammar School in Mt Eden. Mum and Dad's bedroom was upstairs and the kids' rooms were down. There was always plenty going on, lots of the usual squabbling you'd expect among kids. I loved living there and I still love Mt Eden; I love the relaxed feel of it and how it is so easy to just pop down to the village for a coffee. I live there now, in a house that Marisa and I bought in 1998, although we are at the other end of the suburb from my childhood home.

When you're the youngest in a big, busy family like ours, you have to make a lot of noise to get noticed. Sport was one thing where I could hold my own. We had a holiday place at National Park and a bach at Pauanui on the Coromandel Peninsula, so it was water-skiing in summer and snow-skiing in winter. For what seemed like years, I wasn't allowed to go with everyone to Whakapapa skifield because I was too young. When I finally did join them, I was determined not to be left behind. I'd throw myself down the slopes and try to keep up for dear life, although I didn't really know how to ski properly. The same principle applied to everything we did when I was little. I wanted to be able to do what my big brothers and sister were doing.

It felt to me like I grew up at Pauanui. Mum and Dad bought a bach there when I was a toddler. Back then, it was nothing like the developed town of today; just a backwater with a gravel road leading to it. There's an aerial photograph of Pauanui taken around that time and there'd have been barely fifty houses there — a world away from the thousands that are there today. You could get a beachfront section for something like $10,000 — crazy when you look at prices now. We spent many wonderful, long summers there. It was just the best childhood, and the great thing is that Mum and Dad still have a bach by the beach there so the next generation, including my kids, Austin and Phoebe, are getting to enjoy it as much as we did. For me, it was a place where you were free to do just about anything and it was always so much fun.

Although we had a very adventurous life, I'm not sure how much money we actually had. Each year Mum would threaten that things were going to be tight and all we'd be able to afford was mince on toast. My dad, Clive, is a lawyer, a partner in a big firm in Auckland. My mum, Pat, is a teacher. When we were growing up, Dad was establishing himself in his career and worked long hours, so it was Mum who was always around; she was the family rock. I'm a father of two now and I know how busy life can be, but with five kids Mum must have been a bloody legend. Somehow both of them managed to find the time to support us in whatever we did. When I was growing up, they'd always be there whenever I had some event or race.

It must have been a busy life for my parents but that was great for me because I'd be left to roam until it was time to come in for dinner. The evening meal was family time and we'd always sit down together. It was pretty wholesome fare. Mum was big on homemade. Homemade ginger beer, homemade preserves, homemade tomato sauce. Nothing was wasted and we ate very little processed food. Mum's tomato sauce was famous in our household. It was basically water with seeds in it, and when you poured it, it would spread like a lake. Maybe that's why I'm such a fiend for bought tomato sauce now. I put it on everything.

Of course, being kids, we loved the 'bad' stuff. One of my best mates was Chub [Charles George]. We went to kindergarten and primary school together and would hang out at each other's place and ride our bikes around the neighbourhood. I was completely in awe of the fact that there were always chocolate biscuits at his house. I'd ask Chub whether his family actually *ate* biscuits or whether they were just there for show and I'd pig out on them whenever I was round there. I didn't get stuff like that very often at home. Looking back we had an incredibly good diet. There were treats, like fish-and-chip night and goodies that came home with the shopping, but all the choice stuff would get eaten straight away and then we had to survive on the rest until next shopping day.

To me, Pauanui represented fun, adventure and family time. Our first bach there was in a big cul-de-sac. As a preschooler I'd spend hours on end out on my little putt-putt, a plastic trike without pedals, propelling myself along by kicking my legs on the ground. I'd ride on the footpath around the cul-de-sac in a loop that must have been about 800 metres. From the kitchen, Mum and Dad could see me whiz past every ten minutes. Even at that age I worked my legs all the time; I've never been one for sitting still for long.

Pat Carter

As a toddler, all he'd have on would be his towelling hat — no clothes — and he'd be out there most of the day with his little legs going like mad. One time there was a panic when everyone came in for dinner and Hamish, who was eighteen months old, was nowhere to be seen. Clive's mother went off in one direction looking for him, someone went down to the beach, someone else went to the forest, and someone went to the harbour. We found him eventually, still on his circuit but he'd gone up someone's driveway and was using the slope as a ramp to come swooping back down. Hamish was always quite happy with his own company.

One epic day at Pauanui all four Carter boys got up together on water-skis behind the boat. It's a magic moment that's immortalised in a photograph hanging on the bach's toilet wall. I was just shy of ten years old but I remember it clearly because it was such a major undertaking. When the tide was full and conditions were ideal for skiing, the ski lane would be busy. We needed to clear it for the attempt, but that wasn't a problem as everybody knew each other. Word got round that we were having a bash at this great feat and several people came to watch. There were lots of missed attempts; it always seemed that just as the boat started to pull us up someone would fall off. But eventually we made it and did a huge, triumphant lap of the ski lane.

My brother James provided another memorable water-skiing moment when he was about seventeen years old and intent on showing off with a spectacular dismount. The boat brought him towards shore on a massive run-up and James did a big slingshot off the rope to gain maximum speed. Of course, because he was coming in at such speed, everyone sitting on the beach was watching. At a depth of about a foot, he jumped out of his skis and went into a forward flip, but he didn't get around far enough and smashed into the ground, breaking his collarbone. It must have been extremely painful and we really should have felt sorry for him but everyone was laughing their heads off.

As kids we were all quite ballsy. That might have come from our parents and their can-do attitude. For me, wanting to keep up with my brothers definitely spurred me on. There was always another challenge. Once we could water-ski, we had to learn to single ski, and once that was mastered, barefoot skiing was next. I used to love sitting in the boat watching my brothers try that one, because we didn't really know how to do it and there were some horrendous wipeouts. We'd wind the boat up until it was flying and then step out of the skis. Every time someone fell off they'd get absolutely drilled, but they'd always come back for another crack. I took that attitude on board, to always keep trying. It's a sort of toughness, a refusal to quit until you have mastered something.

All of us are sporty. Dad ran cross-country at school and Mum, who grew up in Paraparaumu, was a good roller skater and tennis player. Mum's a pretty tough cookie. She was the originator of many family adventures, such as climbing Mt Pauanui or hiking to some other Coromandel Peninsula vantage point. Dad loved the tramps too, but it was Mum who'd get us cracking — and she didn't have much time for grizzling. If someone complained about being tired and needing a rest, she'd say, 'Well, let's get to the top and you can have a rest up there.' Parts of the trail up Mt Pauanui are like climbing a ladder. It goes up a hundred metres and takes about twenty minutes of solid tramping. We have photos of the whole family on the summit. I would have been seven or eight years old the first time I hiked to the top, and for someone that age it was a big undertaking. I remember walking up that hill and just burning; there are pictures of us wearing nothing but underpants because it was so hot.

On other expeditions we'd take a four-wheel drive into the backblocks and tramp from there. We did a lot of those hikes with family friends, the Hoppers, who developed Pauanui. The Hopper family business has become expert at that sort of coastal lifestyle development around the North Island. Some of those expeditions were very rugged and, being the little guy, it was often hard for me to keep up. Mum says she didn't think I'd survive one time when Ian Hopper, who was a big man, put me on his shoulders and ran off up the river, skipping from boulder to boulder. I loved all these adventures and was just pleased to be included, as there were occasions when I missed out because I was considered too young. The family reckons I didn't take well to being excluded.

Clive Carter

Hamish had a strong personality right from the start. Being the youngest, and boys being boys, he was given a hard time by his brothers and had to learn very quickly to stand up for himself. And he did. He was a nice kid, but he had quite a temper. One time, Pat and

I set off for Fiji. We took the three older children and told Hamish and Tom that we'd take them when they were eleven and safe to swim and go on boats and all the rest of it. Well, Hamish objected strongly to this and my mother, a very fine Christian woman who lived with us, was standing on the front steps seeing us off in the taxi to the airport. Hamish was there too, and as we pulled away he shouted out to us, as loudly as he could, 'Go on then, just fuck off!' My poor mother didn't know whether to cover her ears or his mouth.

Cathy Carter

We did a lot of sporty stuff as a family and Hamish was willing to give everything a go. He must have been only four when we climbed up to the Broken Hill gold mines and I couldn't get over how he would just keep going and going. He was just determined to make it.

Maybe he inherited a bit of Mum's attitude. Being a big family, there wasn't much mollycoddling; everyone was expected to toe the line. At meal times, if you didn't like what was on offer, you had no choice but to sit there until you'd finished it. If you happened to mention that you were a bit tired, Mum would invariably say, 'Oh, you just need to go for a run.' That was her standard response. As she saw it, the problem was that you weren't doing enough.

She was really quite tough with us kids, although not so much with Hamish because she knew he was going to be her last child. The two of them did a lot together. Mum would say, 'Who wants to come shopping?' The rest of us would raise an eyebrow as if to say, 'And why would we?', but off Hamish would go. They had a nice relationship, Hamish and Mum. It wasn't so much that he was the apple of her eye, but rather that she had the time and had chilled out by the time he came along — she had been a young mother.

Although I'm the only one who pursued sport seriously enough to make a career out of it, we all showed some talent. We ran and all the Carter boys played rugby at Saint Kentigern school. I was a lock. I must have been an early developer because I was the tallest in my class at eleven, but that was my peak as far as size went. Cricket bored me, and although I liked rugby, I wasn't that good at it. Generally, I seemed able to do most sports as long as they didn't involve a ball.

I won the cross-country at Saint Kent's and, although I didn't swim much, I was in the school swimming team. I remember winning the eastern zone schools' cross-country on the fields at Macleans College when I was eleven. It was a wet day and I was in bare feet. I was running along in second with not far to go when a teacher screamed at me, 'Sprint, boy!', and I remember thinking, 'Oh, okay'. I put in a burst of speed and passed the boy in front, and won. That was something of a turning point for me because suddenly I realised that I enjoyed it and wondered why I hadn't sprinted like that before.

I definitely enjoyed the buzz I got from winning. At Auckland Grammar if you won something, you were called up on to the stage at assembly. When you're a kid, that's massive. But I didn't consider myself too flash as a runner. I was surprised to do so well in the third form when I finished about sixth at the national schools championships. I remember that trip more for another reason. After the race the older guys took us young ones out and I got absolutely blotto. I was thirteen and it was the first time I'd got drunk. We came close to being expelled. I remember being horrified that, having only just started at Grammar, I was now going to get kicked out. My whole life would be over. In our drunken state we'd wrecked our motel rooms and the owners had complained to the school. I think the teacher in charge of us took the fall and told 'DJ', John Graham, the ex-All Black captain who was headmaster, that it was his fault. It was a scary few days because when you are a third former, secondary school is a big deal. Sad to say, I got in a bit of trouble in those early years.

Although our family is quite academic — what with Mum and Dad's careers — and my brothers all got degrees, that wasn't where my inclinations lay. At Grammar, I was put in 3K, which wasn't good when you consider that the third-form classes were ranked from A to M. It was a brutal system. The letter of your class let everyone know how bright or dumb you were perceived to be. I remember thinking that I was in with a bunch of dummies and that I had to get out if I was going to get anywhere. I worked hard that first year at school and the following year was put up to 4F. That was about the middle of the order and I figured it was good enough for me.

I guess that I cruised a bit from that point and could easily have slipped through the cracks. It was a school where you either made a go of it or you were on the scrap heap. If you weren't the sort who was inclined to put your hand up or get involved in something, you were lost. You had to be a self-starter. Sport became my thing; the only thing I was known for at school. I had no problem grasping the concept that if I trained really hard for a race, I could win it. But for some reason the idea never clicked that if I studied for an exam, I could do well too. Instead, I'd sit in class and wonder what the teacher was talking about.

Mum and Dad were called in by the Dean a couple of times after I failed exams. They tried to encourage me to apply myself but it didn't register. I never thought about needing to make a living, to make money, and about education being the road to that. The only thing that revved me up was seeing sporting heroes, such as when the New Zealand rowing crew visited the school. That blew me away. I thought, 'That's what I want'.

I had tons of friends but rarely went out with them because I was either busy with sport, at Pauanui, or off skiing in the winter. When we did go out, it came as a surprise to see how hard they partied. Sometimes I'd just not drink or I'd go home early. It got to the point where I was sixteen and had no one to take to the school ball. I was a bit of a social loser. All I could see was sport. I guess I had stars in my eyes. If I wasn't rowing, I'd be running in Cornwall Park. I saw John Walker training there a few times and I'd just stop and stare at him. After he'd gone, I'd look at the grass he'd stepped on and think, 'Wow, he was right here'. I'd never met him and I don't know what I would have done if he'd spoken to me. People have said that he wasn't great with the public, or with chatting to kids, but it didn't matter to me. He was the man!

I didn't think I was going to find my future by sitting on my backside with my nose in a book. But somehow I did come to be convinced that sitting on my backside with an oar in my hand would take me somewhere. I got into rowing through my brother, Tom. Grammar had a good rowing programme and Tom made it into the senior rowing eight. A bit of kudos comes with that because rowing is a tough sport. I'm closest in age to Tom — he's three years older — and because he was doing well at rowing, I wanted to row too.

Grammar awarded engraved pewter mugs to the First Rowing Eight. Tom was awarded one in 1986 and I won them in 1988 and 1989. Those mugs still sit on a shelf at the bach. Rowing got into my blood. It wasn't long before I was shooting for the stars and I don't think the family was surprised when sport became my career.

Tom Carter

I enjoy seeing those pewter mugs at the bach. Rowing required an incredible commitment of time and effort, not just for us but for the parents too. One or other of the parents would do the rounds before dawn, picking up sleepy schoolboys from their gates and taking us to training in the silty water of the Tamaki estuary. We'd row through the industrial area of Panmure, past the mangroves, marking our time by the bridges on the route. I'm amazed at the number of people I meet who have rowed. They often talk about wanting to get back in the boat, but life — families, mortgages — gets in the way. There's a bond between rowers, forged out of the adversity they have shared.

Because he's my brother, I don't attach the mystique to Hamish's success that others might, but that doesn't reduce my enjoyment of what he's achieved. He must have something inside him to make him hungrier than the rest because there's a real gritty, mundane side to it. We all have the instinct to do well. My sister Cathy, for example, is a great artist. Hamish made a career out of sport. Everyone in our family has that hunger and desire but in different ways and to different ends.

Doug Carter

I think that the reality with people who become world class is that they are born with special ability. Some people can train as much and try just as hard, but will never make it to the top. Hamish always had something, and so did James. As kids we used to have races, such as the King of the Mountain, where you ran to the top of Pauanui mountain and down again. None of us trained for it. It was a summer holiday event and we'd do it simply on the fitness we had acquired from running around all day long. James and Hame would always win. I'm eight years older than Hamish, but Tom and I would see them at the start and that would be it. They were off.

Dad and I have this theory that there's a freak gene running in the family. Hamish and James have it, and it's in a few of the next generation too. They all behave the same way and even look the same — blonde and chubby, like Hamish and James were as kids. They're phlegmatic kids, lazy, with an 'anything goes' attitude. But once they get going, their diesel engines kick in and they really fire up. As kids, Hamish and James were quiet and very self-contained. They wouldn't run unless they had to, but once they got started, you couldn't stop them.

They were also clever at getting out of chores. We'd all be round the family dinner table having a big discussion, often at volume, about something really important and then it would come time to do the dishes and Hamish and James would have disappeared. They had perfect timing.

TIMING AND BALANCE

Timing and balance. That phrase got drilled into us as young rowers. That's what rowing is all about — besides the blood, sweat and tears, that is. Later I came to understand that it applies to life too. Unless the boat was perfectly balanced, unless the stroke was fluid and perfectly timed, you were never going to get the best out of the boat or crew. It taught me that sport isn't just about grunt and going at it like a bull at a gate. You need to be smooth and efficient.

Grammar's senior eight when I was there was an Under 19 crew. I was 17 and in the sixth form (now called Year 12) when I made it into the First Rowing Eight. I was the stroke, as my brother Tom had been before me. That's the position directly in front of the cox. The rest of the crew sits behind the stroke, who sets the tempo.

Getting the right people in the right seats in an eight is a science in itself. In the middle, you place the strongest rowers, the big grunters. They're the core of the engine room. In rugby terms, they are the locks, the guys who provide the power in the scrum. The bow seat needs a technically proficient rower who the rest can rely on to be error free. Rob Storey, who won an Olympic gold medal and was national rowing manager, explained in a *New Zealand Herald* article that because the bowman is seated behind the others and out of their view, he has to be on top of his game. By nature, he has to be someone who will do the same thing kilometre after kilometre after kilometre, and never vary.

The stroke, my position, is the engine driver, the captain, whose job is to push the team. Storey had this to say about a good stroke: 'He needs to be someone who is half mad, who loves to go, loves to fight, loves to be amongst it at all times and who can instil some of those qualities into the people behind.' Storey cites the example of Tony Hurt, who if you judged 'on ergometer scores, on their ability to run around the block faster than [the rest], you wouldn't pick at all. But he was as tough as old boots, never gave in and hated losing. That's the sort of bloke you put in the stroke seat.'

Tony Hurt was my hero during my rowing days. Hurt was the stroke in the famous gold medal-winning eight at the 1972 Munich Olympics. Grammar's junior eight, which was my first crew, used a beautiful old wooden boat called the *Sir William Stevenson*, named after the civil engineer who developed the engineering materials business William Stevenson & Sons. Wood was a bit past it as race-boat material, even back then in the late 1980s, and we were about the only crew still using a wooden craft. These days they're made of special plastics and materials such as carbon fibre, but this boat was special because of its pedigree. Every time I got in that boat it gave me a buzz. I'd think, 'Wow, I'm sitting in the same seat Tony Hurt sat in'.

My first two years rowing were spent in the Under 17 crew coached by Bryan Goss. Once I had made it into the senior eight, Barry Cleal was my coach. Those guys had a huge impact on me. Goss set the tone for what we were required to do well: you trained hard and you didn't complain. There were no frills about it. Cleal had a quiet way about him, but was one of those guys who could communicate. He was very much to the point and you took what he said on board whether you wanted to hear it or not. 'This is what has to be done. If you want to do it, then let's get on with it. If you don't, then don't come.' That's how it was.

I lived and breathed being a good rower. It wouldn't have mattered what sport I eventually ended up in, rowing instilled the essentials in me: toughness, dependability, respect and playing your part in a team.

They were good old-fashioned values that taught me self-discipline and my place in the world. Mum and Dad gave me that, too, but my rowing days reinforced it in a practical way that I totally related to.

Rowing also taught me about mental toughness, that my body could cope with much more than I thought, that no matter how much I was hurting, I could push a bit more. At training camp, we'd stay on a marae, the rowers sleeping on mattresses in one big room. Day after day we endured huge sessions, and if anyone broke down with injury or lost it mentally they'd be taken to the house where the coaches stayed to be patched up and sent back out again.

It was real tough and I loved it for that reason. You had to learn to suffer. We'd row until our hands bled, but we all did it and we got through it together. Guys would fall asleep at the dinner table, your hands would be so sore you could hardly grip the oar, but you'd have to get back in the boat and row. It was gruesome but it taught me there are no shortcuts to success. It's all hard yakka.

Friends from those rowing days are among my best friends now and that's because we went through so much together. The camaraderie was incredible; you couldn't have got a tighter bunch. That doesn't mean we didn't have blow-ups — even punch-ups — when the pressure was at its most intense before a big race, but we always pulled together when it mattered. I have massive respect for rowers because I know what they go through. I've never suffered pain as acute as I did in a rowing race. Guys would be spewing from the effort.

When I switched to triathlon I was amazed when someone in my swim squad complained to the coach about being tired — and I was shocked when the coach reduced his workload. I couldn't believe the way triathletes talked back, and that the workout might be negotiable. In rowing, the coaches set the work and you gave total commitment each time you got in the boat or you were sent home. Olympic swimmer Danyon Loader always referred to his coach, Duncan Laing, as Mr Laing. It was the same with our rowing coaches.

Barry Cleal was one of those coaches who made you want to achieve. He had a way of drawing the best from you. We won a lot of races, but the Maadi Cup was the big one. I wanted to win that as much for my coach as myself.

Rowing was on the banks of mainstream sport. Rugby, cricket and soccer were the main codes at Grammar. I wasn't interested in trying to get into the first XV; it just seemed too rock star-ish. It might sound crazy, but because so many people seemed good at rugby, I wondered whether it could really be that hard. On the other hand, rowing in the Maadi Cup is one of the toughest things I've done. Just making the eight was an achievement, let alone reaching the final. Racing that regatta set so many things straight within me. It made me realise what I wanted.

The Maadi is the Holy Grail for New Zealand schoolboy rowers. It's like going to the Olympics when you're 17. Grammar had never won the Maadi Cup and we were the school's big hope. We got beaten two years running by Christ's College. The first time we lost was the worst day of my life. So was the second time. I hated it but I also realised how close we'd come to reaching the top of that mountain. The first time was particularly frustrating because we had a weak link in the boat, but the second time we rowed really well and were beaten by a better crew. In those circumstances, it makes you a bit more accepting of the result.

The most valuable lesson I learned from my rowing coaches was about timing and balance. It became a mantra for me and, although back then it was in reference to getting the boat to go fast, I have built my career around it. It made me a thinking athlete, and, as I've already said, it's just as relevant to life in general. If you have timing and balance in whatever you do, you'll succeed, because that's what everything comes down to. As rowers, a crew obviously needs to be in time and the boat needs to be balanced. You need a balanced diet, but you need a balanced life too — to know when to work and when to relax. It sounds simple but it's hard to get right.

Timing is obviously important in racing — knowing the moment to make the big effort — but it also applies to training. It's like putting together a big jigsaw puzzle. Anyone can race brilliantly at some point during a season but winning is about being able to produce your peak performance on the day it counts most. Over-train and you may peak too early and be flat for the big day; under-train and you won't be at your best in time.

The professional triathletes on the world circuit are like the single-scullers of rowing. They're on their own and completely responsible for themselves. They're not the sort to party all the time, although we do have a blowout or two during the year after a major race. You can't be a party animal if you want to produce consistent results, and without consistency you aren't going to be very successful. I could never understand it when I'd read about rugby players going on benders for days on end, as some from North Harbour reportedly did after winning the 2006 Ranfurly Shield. They went on to lose game after game. Didn't they want to go out and prove again that they were the best? Doing it once doesn't mean anything.

Clive and Pat Carter

Hamish was told by his rowing coach, Barry Cleal, that he would represent New Zealand at something. I think it was because of his stamina. He used to out-erg the others, or whatever the expression is, even though he wasn't as big. It was a comment that must have stuck in his head. We noticed it. He had the ambition to do well in sport.

Barry Cleal

It may be nearly 20 years ago but I well remember the Carter boys. Tom was the trendsetter. They both stroked and they were both at the Maadi in the same year: Tom in the senior eight and Hamish in a junior crew coached by Bryan Goss. Hamish's crew won.

Grammar had a good rowing history but had been in a slump. Hamish's group was at the beginning of a renaissance. They twice finished second in the Maadi Cup senior eight, but that wouldn't have meant anything to Hamish. Coming second wasn't an option to him. The big thing about the Maadi, is that it's *The Maadi*. You can talk to people about it years later and they don't even tell you whether they won, they just say with an excited look on their face, 'I was in the Maadi.' That was the thing. They were good enough to represent their school and have a seat in that eight for that row.

John Graham was headmaster during that rowing revival and he and the late Ian McKinley, his deputy, and Des Cutler, who's known as the father of Grammar rowing, played a significant part. John Graham would talk to the crew before they travelled to the Maadi. To be able to listen to those talks was a privilege. He'd tell them that if they turned out their best result, then it was gold, even if they didn't win the race. One year, he talked about leading the All Blacks to what was then the team's worst loss. 'But I was still proud to be an All Black,' he told them. You could see these kids grow taller as they listened, and when they walked out of his office they were walking on clouds.

The Carters lived next door to the school. The parents were chalk and cheese. Clive, a lawyer, was statesman-like, quiet and hugely full of pride; the mother, Pat, was a real neat, bossy little schoolteacher. Hamish and Tom were encouraged to be independent, given a bit of freedom, allowed to make a few mistakes, although they didn't get into any real trouble. John Graham kept an eye on them because, I guess, they were just plain bloody mischievous. Life was an absolute dream to both of them. They loved life and were full of curiosity. They were two boys who automatically smiled, even when they were nearly crying.

It's no surprise to me that Hamish has done well. He had a winning attitude; he set an example without trying to. You know that smile he has on his face the whole time? I'd load up the crew with heavy work and he'd get this look as if to say 'Bring it on'. I never did see him crack, never saw any sign that he might. His cardiovascular fitness was 100 per cent. He was a lightweight guy with a heavyweight heart.

Although life revolved around rowing, I still ran, mostly in the off season. It was good for my cardiovascular fitness but might have been more hindrance than help for rowing because good runners are light and lithe, whereas top rowers are big, strong guys. Dad had been captain of the Wellington Boys' cross-country team and I ran because, although he never actually said it, I knew he wanted me to.

I won the intermediate steeplechase, the Clements Cup, in my second year at Grammar and later won the senior 1500 metres (the Donald Lane Cup) and twice won the Maxwell Cronin Cup for the open steeplechase. Cross-country is an aerobic sport, whereas rowing is anaerobic, so twice a year I'd retrain my body to switch the way it converted and used energy, as well as losing weight for running and then putting it back on when it was time to pick up the oars. By running cross-country each winter I was unwittingly putting in the core conditioning that assured my future as a triathlete.

I didn't spend all my time in class daydreaming about rowing. Just most of it. The school was very generous about my academic ability. A little bio they wrote about me much later as 'old boy of the year' following the Athens Olympics reads: 'Although Hamish was a standout athlete, he also performed well academically, coming first in his class as a third former and second as a sixth former.' Mercifully, they didn't mention that academic first was in 3K.

I think I had enough smarts to do okay academically if that had been my goal, but my first Maadi Cup sealed it for me. Rowing was to be my route to becoming a world champion. And I wanted to be in the best rowing crew in the world.

Not long after leaving school, the omens turned against me. I stopped growing. I'm 1.81 m and naturally light. I'd bulk up to 74 kg by pigging out during my annual break from triathlon training but I've been as light as 67 kg, which was my weight at the Athens Olympics. The optimal size for a rower is closer to 1.9 m and 95 kg — about the dimensions of Olympic champion sculler Rob Waddell. It wouldn't have mattered how much I tried to transform myself, genetics was against me.

I was studying engineering and building management at polytech and had joined Auckland Rowing Club, which had a strong association with Grammar, when I got put out of the stroke seat. I was moved to number four, the side of the boat that requires more technique than strength. Tony Hurt was a small dude too and he had stroked the best crew in the world, so I'd thought that I could do it. But as soon as I lost the stroke seat, I knew that was it. The decision was made by Peter Abbott. He was a bloody good coach and it made perfect sense. I was lucky to keep a seat in the crew. We won the senior eight that year at the national champs but I knew I was on borrowed time. I kept rowing for a couple of months but felt like a punctured balloon. I was told that I had a big future in lightweight rowing — the Under 72 kg division — but my heart was no longer in it. If I was going to be the best at rowing, it had to be against all comers. I needed to find a sport where I could excel unconditionally.

Barry Cleal

Had there been another outstanding lightweight for Hamish to row with he'd have gone to the top, international class, no doubt in my mind. He had what it took. The Grammar crews would do this 11-day camp at Mangakino. It was blatant over-training but there was no other way to get the work in. We would monitor the boys' resting heart rate each morning as an indication of how they were coping. A significant increase indicated that the training was knocking them around and they needed more recovery time. Hamish's heart rate would go up a couple of beats during the camp whereas the others would be up 10 or more. He was so fit that the hard training didn't affect him as much.

A good stroke needs tenacity, personality and natural rhythm. You can't create that and Hamish had it. But, ultimately, his weight became an insurmountable problem. It's just the way the dice rolls. Hamish found a better pathway.

Even though I idolised John Walker, running didn't strike me as a viable alternative. I considered myself a rower who could run and didn't have the same passion for it. Then, like fate, triathlon fell in my lap.

I knew a little about the sport because I was going out with a triathlete, Alex Stewart, and then one day I went for a swim at Panmure's Swimarama pool and saw a flyer on the noticeboard for its triathlon squad. Triathlon sounded like fun — sun, surf, barbecues on the beach — so I turned up the next day and joined the squad.

One of my first events was at Whangamata during the summer of 1990–91. I was cocky and contemptuous. I figured that rowers were the toughest of the tough, so triathlon would be a piece of cake. Time hasn't dimmed my memory of being passed by girls on the hilly bike leg. The race took two hours, not the six minutes I was used to from rowing. I completely disintegrated after half an hour on the bike and even thought about pulling out. The results show that I finished seventh, which doesn't sound too bad, but in reality I got severely dealt to. Even so, I was hooked. One day I was a rower, the next I was a triathlete.

A DUCK TO WATER

During the early '90s in the world of triathlon, Rick Wells was King Kong, and if there can be such a thing as Queen Kong, her name was Erin Baker. Rick is a farmer's son from Te Aroha and Erin is from a sporty Christchurch family. Kiwis have done well in this sport almost from its birth.

There's a story about triathlon having evolved from a bet made in a bar to solve an argument about which athlete from what sport was superior. The consensus seems to be that the first triathlon was held in San Diego in 1974, when I was three years old. The famous endurance triathlon, the Ironman (3.2 km swim, 180 km bike and full marathon of 42.2 km) was born in Hawaii four years later. That race captured the imagination of the Americans and later the Europeans, probably because it's so gruelling. The race was dominated by Americans for 16 years and made legends of Dave Scott, Mark Allen, Scott Tinley and Scott Molina, who were known as the Big Four.

In 1989, the International Triathlon Union (ITU) was founded in Avignon, France, and the first official world championships were held. Since then, the sport has grown like mad and spread around the globe, with more than 100 affiliated national federations. The official distance was set at a 1500 m swim, a 40 km cycle and a 10 km run, drawn from existing Olympic events, and is referred to as the 'standard' or 'Olympic' distance. That's the one I concentrated on. It's the distance of the ITU World Cup series, as well as the Olympic and Commonwealth Games.

Triathlon made its debut in my hometown, Auckland, at the 1990 Commonwealth Games where it had 'demonstration sport' status. Wells and Baker both won in front of a huge and patriotic crowd. I didn't see the race because I was at rowing training. They were already world champions but those wins underlined the fact that Kiwis were talented at this young sport.

I suspect it has something to do with our No 8 wire heritage. We're renowned for our adaptability and that's what you need in an event where three sports are combined. You have to be able to deal with the fact that they are contrary disciplines; swimmers generally can't run, runners can't bike, and cyclists aren't known for taking to the water like ducks. You need to be able to adapt, to work on your weaknesses and find the right balance. It takes understanding, perseverance and bucket-loads of hard work.

Erin Baker had all that in spades. You would be hard pressed to find anyone who trained harder or was mentally tougher. Some of her male training partners are reputed to have made themselves scarce when she was doing particularly hard sessions because they were afraid of getting hammered.

Erin was probably the most complete female triathlete. She won world titles across a range of distances, was also world duathlon (run-bike-run) champion twice and won some big road running races in the United States. It's not surprising then that she was the first non-American (male or female) to be named world Triathlete of the Year.

When I arrived in the sport in 1992, the men's benchmark was set by Rick Wells. Although he was nearing the end of his career, he remained dominant. Rick's background was in swimming, in which he represented New Zealand at Commonwealth Games level. He trained with his friend Graeme Miller, an Olympic cyclist, and had also become a very good runner. He had the total package needed for triathlon, and by the time I started racing he had won world championships over both the standard and long-course distances. He was a star and I wanted nothing more than to beat him.

Once I started training specifically for triathlons I began to do well and even won some small races. That gave me instant feedback that I had potential and it spurred me on. Within a year I was lining up at the New Zealand Championships in New Plymouth, with Mum and Dad there watching. I didn't really have any expectations. All the top triathletes were racing, most of whom I hadn't beaten.

Wells was clearly still at the top of his game. Four months earlier, in October 1991, he'd come second equal at the world champs, out-sprinted by a young Australian named Miles Stewart — an athlete with whom I would have many battles in the coming years. Tony O'Hagan, Scott Ballance, John Hellemans, Jackson Foster and Walter Thorburn were among the top older guys and there was a group of young guns known as 'the brat pack' that included Jamie Hunt, Cameron Brown, Paul Amey, Brendon Downey, David Lee, Richard Wagner and Nick Spragg. There was serious depth in the sport.

I didn't really appreciate what I was up against. Wells emerged from the water in the lead with O'Hagan, a strong cyclist, chasing. I was with a big group of riders behind them. The group got caught behind a milk tanker (this was before courses were closed to traffic), which caused chaos in the bunch. I had the rower's mindset — each time the oar went in the water was your chance to move the boat faster — and I applied that to my cycling. Each pedal stroke was an opportunity to move away from the opposition. I thought 'bugger this' and pulled onto the wrong side of the road, passed the tanker and went for it.

I finished fourth but won the bronze medal because an American crossed the line third and non-residents were ineligible as far as championship placings went. The American turned out to be Scott Molina, one of the Big Four. His nickname was The Terminator, earned because of his reputation as one of triathlon's tough guys. I didn't know much about the history of my new sport, and had no idea that for most of the run I was stride for stride with one of its rock stars. Molina is a good guy. He married Erin Baker and they live in

Christchurch with their two kids. He's still involved in the sport, does the odd race and helps to coach Cameron Brown, who has become one of the world's best Ironman triathletes.

Back then, the only triathletes I knew were Rick Wells and this group of young brat-pack athletes who I saw winning a lot of races around the North Island. I'd heard about a top American having entered and I figured the guy who caught me on the run must be him because he made a couple of helpful comments, such as telling me to cut the corners, and I noticed that he had an accent. After the race people were in awe: 'Wow, you were running with Scott Molina!' And my response was: 'Who's he?'

My ignorance probably helped because no matter who I was with in a race, all I wanted to do was get away from them. During the race I'd thought, 'Well, if it is this guy he can't be that good because I'm running with him. And, besides, I'm gonna beat him.' That was my arrogance again. Anyway, Molina beat me by eight seconds, but I couldn't have been more rapt. Behind me was a line-up of top guys, including all the brat pack, who I had never beaten before. And I'd never got as close to Wells either. I was just 43 seconds behind him.

I saw Mum and Dad soon after I crossed the line and I'll never forget the look of joy and disbelief on their faces. Although I'd been a good rower, the result was beyond all our expectations. Suddenly, I'd won a national medal and was named in the elite team to represent New Zealand at the world champs in Muskoka, Canada. Cripes! Apart from a family holiday to the Pacific Islands, I'd never been overseas before.

I loved that Mum and Dad got a buzz out of it, and the fact that people close to me got such a kick out of it when I did well became a driving force for me. Not that anyone goes on about it. Mum and Dad are very quiet about that sort of thing, as is the whole family. No one is put on a pedestal. That's very grounding, and it didn't change when I became successful internationally. The family was overjoyed when I won in Athens, and my brother James, who lives in Sydney, suggested a family night to celebrate. We got together in Auckland and at dinner we talked about the Olympics for around five minutes or so and then moved on. That's great because, although I'm writing this book, I'm not one to dwell on what I have done. The coolest thing about our family is that no matter what anyone has done, life goes on. Mum and Dad's attitude was, 'Be there, enjoy it, but don't make a big deal about things'.

Clive Carter

Hamish's result at the 1992 national championships was a surprise. For the first time the thought crossed our minds that this triathlon thing might go somewhere. Rick Wells was the favourite and he was famous. For Hamish to be there, pushing him, was really something. Rick set it off for Hamish. He became Hamish's measuring stick for everything.

I started to win races after that bronze medal and later that year I beat both Rick and Tony O'Hagan for the first time. My progress coincided with Wells' career coming to an end. He'd lost a bit of his drive, though that didn't enter my head at the time. I just wanted to kick his arse every moment I was in a race against him, but at the same time I never really thought that I would. When it happened, it changed my life because it suddenly gave me belief. If I beat him — a world champion — then I was capable of beating anyone. That's the way my logic worked. Had it not been for him, I might never have gone overseas to chase my dream of being the best.

That breakthrough happened at the 1992 national duathlon championships. Although I won the race, Rick withdrew early, during the bike leg. The newspaper quoted him as saying that he wasn't mentally prepared. These days we get on really well. It can't have been easy trying to fend off all of us young pretenders. I got a taste of that later when I became the sport's elder statesman.

One of the things that made triathlons so popular in the early years was that the stars lined up beside everyone else. It didn't matter that you were just a weekend warrior, you could be waiting for the starting gun next to Rick Wells or Erin Baker, and get to race alongside them (if only for 10 seconds). It's that way now in the Stroke & Stride, a weekly swim-run event held in Auckland at St Heliers during summer, and at Xterra, the cross-country version of triathlon.

After Rick retired, I'd periodically get an email or text from him after races saying 'Well done' or, if things hadn't gone my way, 'Don't worry about it, the sun will still come up tomorrow'. He even gave me good advice when I was his rival, which says a lot about the sort of person he is. When I broke my collarbone in the French Alps in 1994, he told me not to let it get me down because if that was the worst to happen in my career I'd have escaped lightly.

Rick Wells

> During the nationals in New Plymouth, this kid came flying past on the bike. He had longish blond hair and looked a bit like US rock singer Tom Petty. I thought, 'Who the hell is that?' I managed to peg him back during the run, but it took some doing. That's my earliest recollection of young Mr Carter. I didn't get to know him until after I'd retired. Back then he was a cocky kid. There was a whole bunch of them coming through and he wasn't one of the stars among them. Cameron Brown and Paul Amey were the standouts. From my perspective, Amey was the most talented. He had talent to burn and that's basically what he did with it. He was a fast swimmer and he could run as fast as anyone — 29 minutes for 10 km. He's one guy who I think didn't make the most of his talent.
>
> The great thing about Hamish is how he developed the natural ability he had. He wasn't a great swimmer, but he worked on it and made swimming his strength. His running was okay rather than brilliant, but he's worked methodically on that too and got the results. It's hard to have a friendship with someone you're racing against, but there was admiration and respect there even then.

After my surprise medal at the national triathlon champs, I decided there and then that I wanted to be a professional athlete. I'd been offered a job in the construction industry the Friday before that race and I'd intended to take it, but that result changed everything. Suddenly I went from thinking it was neat to do well in races at home, to deciding that I had to go overseas and take up the sport as a profession. I knew there was prize money to be had and figured that if I did well, I could survive.

I was living at home with Mum and Dad and it must have been

tough for them when I announced that I was turning down the job, but they never tried to talk me out of it. They supported whatever I wanted to do. They might suggest I should have something as a back-up, perhaps be a builder as Mum's father had been, but they never once said that I shouldn't go after my dream.

Clive Carter

Hamish told us he wanted to try to make a career in triathlon. We didn't have a problem with that, even though his brothers went to university and were quite academic. We could see that Hamish had some sort of skill and we remembered his teachers at Grammar, who had also thought he would make it in sport. I used to say to Pat that he would definitely make it in something, though who knew what that might be.

Pat Carter

As a parent you feel that it would be good for your child to have something as a backstop. His friend, Chub, did building management and Hamish started off doing that at tech with him. He lasted a year, but his heart wasn't in it.

In August 1992, I boarded a plane for the United States and flew off alone on my first foray into the big wide world. My parents were at the airport to wave goodbye. I was terrified about leaving behind my family and support network, everything that was familiar to me. Even as I walked through the departure gate, I was thinking, 'What am I doing?' I was stepping out into the unknown, and I felt afraid and excited at the same time.

I was bound for Santa Cruz, California, to take up the offer of accommodation from Krista Whelan. I'd met at the Ironman in Auckland. Here I was, at 21, on my first real trip overseas, trying to negotiate foreign airports with 10 bags in tow — a bike bag, wheel bags and other gear bags. I made mistake after mistake. For a start, I failed to register the difference between currencies and spent most of my cash on stuff that I thought was a real bargain. Talk about green.

Fortunately, it was a short trip. The plan was to do the last part of my preparation for the world championships in the United States before flying on to Muskoka, in Canada. Another mistake was doing an extra race just one week out from the worlds. I hadn't intended to, but the girl I was staying with was doing the race and invited me along to watch. Once we got to San Francisco, someone suggested doing it, and I thought, 'Why not?'

The 'Escape from Alcatraz' is famous for the unique nature of the course. It's also bloody tough, as I discovered. It starts with a swim from the island's notorious old prison site in San Francisco Bay. Typical of my lack of preparation at the time, I didn't know anything about the course. I thought I'd just follow everyone else. I'd assumed that it was a standard-distance course, finishing, as usual, with a 10 km run on sealed roads. Not only was the run 18 km, but it was on rough hilly trails. Hardly ideal preparation when you're supposed to be resting up for a world championship race. To make matters worse, I hadn't told my coach, Jack Ralston, that I was doing it.

I thought it was the coolest race. We swam from Alcatraz to the mainland, and the next thing I knew I was biking over the famous Golden Gate bridge. It was wicked. I was gawking around oohing and ahhing, more like a tourist than a serious athlete. The funny thing was that I was in second place at the end of the bike section. People were wondering who this unknown guy was, and I heard the announcer suggesting I might have taken a wrong turn (in other words, a shortcut). Then they found out I was from New Zealand, but somehow got the idea that I'd just flown in that morning from halfway around the world. They were going nuts, talking about this young Kiwi freak. After the race I tried to explain that I'd been in Santa Cruz for two weeks but they didn't want that story. They loved the idea that I'd just flown in.

The buzz I felt during the bike wore off when the run wandered off into the wilderness. By the time I'd run 10 km I was knackered. Then I heard a voice behind me say, 'Hey man, who are you?' I got a hell of a shock because I recognised the guy's blond hair and wispy moustache. It was Scott Tinley, one of the Big Four. I battled on to the finish and got fourth, a result that was greeted with general amazement.

Man, did I put my foot in it after the race. Because I was an unknown, the media was quite interested in me and kept asking whether I was surprised to have done so well. I had no experience with talking to the media and, being young and arrogant, I called it as I saw it. The current world Olympic-distance champion was an Australian, while Wells, a double world champion, was a Kiwi. To me, the power base was in Australasia, and I told them so fairly bluntly. No, I said, I wasn't surprised at how well I'd done because Americans weren't very good at triathlon. Oops. Not a smart thing to say in the country that invented triathlon and had produced the Big Four.

Everyone knew who I was after that — that cocky kid from New Zealand. It was all over the magazines and I'm still periodically reminded about it by the Americans, most recently at the 2006 Xterra World Championship in Hawaii — 15 years later! Well, you live and learn. And that's what I did at Muskoka.

Two days later, I flew to Buffalo on the American–Canadian border en route to Muskoka, and found myself sitting next to basketball hero Magic Johnson. The excitement soon wore off when I landed and discovered there was a conference in Buffalo and not a room to be had anywhere. Stranded at the airport with all my bags and nowhere to sleep, I opted to bus the rest of the way. After 10 hours, the bus dropped me in the downtown bus depot in Toronto. There were freaks and geeks and, I was sure, a few mass murderers hanging around that place. I was convinced I'd get killed or my $5000 bike would get nicked if I hung around. I got in the first taxi I saw and told the driver to take me to an expensive hotel. I got picked up from there later by the New Zealand team.

Looking back, I wonder what I was thinking. I'd convinced myself I was invincible, and despite Alcatraz and that journey, I still thought I could do well in the race. As it turned out, Hellemans was best placed of the senior New Zealand men in 20th. Rick was 23rd and I was 61st — nearly last. It was like someone had pulled the rug out from under me. But it was good for me because it made me think I wasn't that special after all. I realised I'd have to work harder.

The trip was a great experience, if not financially rewarding. Back home, the fact that I was broke and jobless didn't bother me too much because I was living with Mum and Dad who gave me a tow financially and, at times, literally. I was driving a clapped-out Volkswagen Beetle and needed rescuing on more than one occasion.

On my return, I threw myself into the local triathlon season and started winning. At one stage, I took out something like 18 races in a row. The City of Auckland Triathlon, which I won by a good margin from O'Hagan, was a big deal because it was the most important race I'd won. Looking back at the newspaper clipping, I see that the event was significant for something else too. 'Marisa Pentecost also gained her first major win in only her second season in the sport,' reads the race report. I didn't know her then, but I do now. She's my wife.

I won both the New Zealand Olympic and Sprint (750 m swim, 20 km bike, 5 km run) titles in January 1993 and set my sights on tackling the Aussies in the Queensland Championship on the Gold Coast. It was the final race of a prestigious series and their top guys were racing, including Miles Stewart. I don't know whether they were too busy watching each other or they didn't rate me, but I biked away from them and won. I was as surprised as they were.

Greg Bennett, Australian Olympian

> That Gold Coast race was the first time I saw Hamish. I finished about 10th and remember thinking, 'Whoa, here's this Kiwi guy not long in the sport and he rolls up and wins'. I was a youngster then and assumed he was some older guy. Later I found out we were the same age. It was a lesson for me. I needed to pick up my game.

That turned out to be an important race because I was invited to join a group of Australian triathletes, coached by Brett Sutton, who were heading to the south of France to train and race. It was another quantum leap for me. Going to America had been the biggest thing and now I was off to France. Sutton had a reputation for setting punishing training schedules and producing world-beaters. It was going to be interesting.

I'd been winning one or two thousand dollars per race over summer and because I was living at home had managed to save enough for a return ticket to Europe and a couple of months' accommodation.

I had no sponsorship, so I needed to win prize money if I were to stay longer.

I was still a novice when it came to travelling, but I got myself to Paris and then on the TGV to Grenoble, at the foot of the French Alps. Our base was in Alpe d'Huez, a town at the top of the climb made famous by the Tour de France. It's a brute, with 21 switchback corners and later I became one of its victims.

Alpe d'Huez is remote; there's just nothing there. I was staying with a group of athletes I didn't know, in shitty accommodation, in a country where I couldn't understand what people were saying. In addition, I didn't really know where I was. I wouldn't have been able to point out Grenoble on the map, let alone Alpe d'Huez. It was like I'd stepped off planet Earth. It's fair to say that I was pretty spooked.

The first night, I walked down the street to a phone booth (there was no phone at the accommodation) and rang my brother Doug, who was living in London. I wanted to hear a familiar voice. I'm the sort that gets homesick, and Doug sensed that I was freaked. He sent me a fax the next day telling me to have a good time. 'If it turns to shit, just come over here.' That made the difference. The fact that I had an escape route gave me the confidence to stay. If I didn't like it, I could go to Doug's, and if things really didn't work out, I could just go home.

The first race we went to was an eight-hour drive away in the poxy van we'd rented. We tried to squeeze into one hotel room but a couple of guys had to sleep in the van. It was pretty full on, but fun too. The swim was in a lake and we started on a nudist beach. Most were old people but there were quite a few topless girls of about 18 or 19, too. I thought it was awesome. In fact, I missed the start because I was too busy having a good look around.

I didn't have a particularly stunning race but I won some prize money. Numbers were the first French words I learnt and this time I didn't repeat the exchange rate mistake I'd made in America. I knew what the purse was for each placing and I ran along trying to catch the person in front of me to pick up a few hundred dollars more. I finished third or fourth, won some money and was on my way.

I managed to earn enough from racing to stay three months, right through to the world championships in Manchester in August, which had been my plan. Mum and Dad were coming over to watch, so that was an incentive to stick it out in France. The homesickness didn't disappear, but I began to enjoy myself more.

I was with a good bunch of guys and we had lots of laughs. Getting to races invariably involved long road trips, and as the budget was tight, we had the tinniest rental vehicles. That was probably a blessing because they got trashed. There'd be bikes and wheels and people jammed inside right up to the roof. One rental blew its motor during a seven-hour drive to a race in some small town.

That particular race was significant for me because I won, breaking the course record. The French media went a bit crazy about that because the record belonged to England's Simon Lessing and he was a big name in triathlon. Lessing went on to win the world championships four times.

Those months with Sutton's group gave me a harder edge. Sutton was old school, a real hard-arse in his approach to coaching. He wanted to smash his athletes in training and get them as fit as possible. He burnt some out, but he made others world class. He was a bit of a nutcase who was famous for his crazy sessions. One involved 40 repeat efforts of 400 m, which is a huge workload. To make it tougher, Sutton would make them do some of the repetitions wearing wetsuits.

At first I was worried that he was going to destroy me, but I had my own training programme from my coach, Jack Ralston, back in Auckland and made it clear from the beginning that I would pretty much be doing my own thing. I did train with the others, but it meant that I could opt out of anything I thought wasn't right for me. As I got to know Sutton better, I'd ask his advice more and he helped me a lot, particularly in understanding what was required at the top level. Biking up Alpe d'Huez certainly strengthened my cycling. Those months in France lifted me to another level.

I knew I was in good shape but I didn't have any specific expectations for the world champs. Naturally, I wanted to do as well as I could in front of my family. As well as my parents, Doug, his English partner, Abbey, and her parents, and my sister, Cathy, and her partner, Paul, were also coming to Manchester to cheer me on. It was great to join the New Zealand team and be among Kiwis again. The squad included Natasja Hilgeholt, who was my girlfriend, and Marisa, who was in the elite team.

This is how the New Zealand Press Association reported the race: 'Carter showed the benefit of his European-based racing season in finishing third behind Britons Spencer Smith and Simon Lessing. Carter emerged from the 1.5 km swim in the chilly Rivington Reservoir about 10th in a large group that included New Zealand's former world champion Rick Wells. Unlike Wells, who faded on the 40 km cycle and later withdrew, Carter rode strongly and was second, just 37 seconds down on race leader Smith at the end of the leg.'

Smith was younger than me. He'd won the junior world title the year before and Lessing was the reigning world champion. I was trying to hold on during the run and was second until two-thirds of the way through when Lessing passed me. Brad Beven, a Queenslander who was becoming a big star, was closing in on me, and Ben Bright from my Alpe d'Huez training group was in fifth place, so I was in pretty exalted company. There's a photo of me coming down the finishing chute with a look of sheer disbelief on my face.

Cathy

The lake was really cold. It was grey and wet, and they raced along little, winding cobblestone lanes. It was the first time I'd seen him competing and I was worried about him taking the corners because it was so slippery.

Doug

It was a great atmosphere, very exciting. My parents-in-law are not sporty at all and didn't know what a triathlon was, but they came along to watch and got into it, especially with Hamish doing so well. Hamish had stayed at their home and had demolished their fridge, devouring everything in sight, and they'd been quite bemused by how someone so skinny could eat so much. A good mate of mine from Auckland, Al Munro, was with us. After one of the favourites passed Hamish during the run, Al sprinted alongside Hame and said 'You'd better hold on to third or your mother's gonna kill you!'

Pat and Clive

> The result came absolutely out of the blue. We used to get severe attacks of nerves watching him. You try not to get your hopes too high, but then, if things don't work out, you feel bitterly disappointed for him because you know what he'd put into it.

That result brought me instant recognition. It was like a lightning strike. Suddenly people knew who I was. While I was staying with Doug, after the worlds, I noticed in a triathlon magazine that there was a World Cup race coming up in Maui. I'd never been to Hawaii and thought it would be neat to do the race on my way home to Auckland. The problem was that I'd missed the entry deadline. I didn't hold much hope of getting a start but rang the race director anyway. He asked who I was and I couldn't believe the response when I told him. 'Sure,' he said, 'we've got you a hotel and there'll be a car at the airport to meet you.'

Two weeks after the world championships, I finished second to Brad Beven in the Paris International Triathlon, gathered up my entourage of gear bags and headed to the airport. The hotel in Hawaii was on the edge of the ocean and in the huge foyer was an enormous water feature with real pink flamingos. It was like something out of *The Lives of the Rich and Famous* and there I was, in shorts and jandals, with my mouth gaping and all my travel-worn bags strewn around me. It was one hell of a contrast to the cramped, frugal, unglamorous existence I'd been leading in France. 'Damn,' I thought, 'this is a bit of alright!'

The race was a bit of alright, too. My first World Cup start and I won. It was a neat way to end my first proper international season. I flew home on a high. Those last three races — Manchester (third), Paris (second) and Hawaii (first) — put me on the map. A big Japanese triathlon magazine ran a feature on me under the headline, 'The Next One'. I was being talked about as a star-in-waiting.

CRASH AND BURN

My dream run continued after I got home. I had a few races and won them all. They included the national sprint-distance championships in Dunedin but, more importantly, the national Olympic-distance championships in Wellington, on the course to be used for the world champs later in 1994.

The worlds in Wellington was my big goal; my aim was to better the bronze I won in Manchester by becoming world champion at the first triathlon world championships to be held in New Zealand. The nationals were a great chance to get a feel for the course and it meant something to me, too, that I beat Rick Wells into second. He'd been in the field in Manchester, but finishing ahead of him in Wellington felt more like the real thing because we raced head to head in front of a home crowd. I had a lead of 30 seconds on him by the end of the bike and extended that to almost a minute at the finish.

I'd made a lot of progress in 12 months but it still came as a surprise to be named Rookie of the Year for 1993 by the respected US magazine *Triathlete*. Its senior editor, Jeffrey Justice, wrote that in other years it had been hard to pick a winner but this time it wasn't even close. I was following in some pretty big footsteps. Previous winners included former world champion Miles Stewart, and Lance Armstrong, who went on to dominate the Tour de France.

Although I was getting a reputation in the triathlon world, what made me a familiar face in New Zealand households was a television programme called *Clash of the Codes.* The programme was conceived by Paul MacDonald — one half of the Ferg and Macka duo — who dominated Olympic kayaking with Ian Ferguson during the 1980s. He decided it would make great television to get teams from a variety of sports and test them in a series of events that required speed, strength and endurance. It was a battle between the sports to find which athletes were superior. It was probably one of the first reality television shows and it was a hit, both ratings-wise and with those involved. I had a ball.

The series was filmed during an 11-day stretch and it was like living in a circus populated by elite athletes. We stayed at the Sheraton Hotel and for some it was a constant party. After competing and filming all day, we'd spend the evenings living it up. There was always a group in the hotel spa pool who would order tray after tray of beers. I joined in the fun, but I've never been much of a drinker. In the triathlon team, that responsibility fell to Wellsie, who was well qualified for the role. Each team had one female athlete; ours was Erin Christie.

Being a new discipline, triathlon was regarded as a fringe sport and lacked some credibility in the eyes of those from long-established codes, so I was keen to show we were good athletes. Although it was definitely fun, everyone competed like crazy to show their sport in the best light. Living together in the one hotel made it even more intense, and there were rows and tantrums. I remember cyclist Graeme Miller, who's as feisty a competitor as you could meet, going berserk at Paul MacDonald during one event when something happened to his team's jet ski. Grown men would just scream at each other.

A lot of high-profile sports people were involved: All Blacks Zinzan Brooke and Ant Strachan, Kiwi rugby league international Richie Blackmore, and Sandra Edge from the Silver Ferns. I was more nervous in the *Clash of the Codes* competitions than for some of my triathlon races.

Our team had a cunning plan. While Erin and I went to bed at a reasonable hour to make sure we were on top of our game, Wellsie would take our rivals out drinking, getting some so written off they could hardly get on the bus the next morning. It was hilarious.

Midway through the competition, teams in the bottom half of the field were eliminated. That meant added pressure if you were close to the cut. One event involved a mountain-bike ride up a very steep hill somewhere out by Auckland's west coast beaches. It was originally intended to be a downhill race but MacDonald decided the track was so steep that someone was bound to kill themselves.

At this point in the competition, the cyclists were in danger of being eliminated but this event was made for them. So I was puzzled when Miller asked us to let them win and promised they'd repay the debt by helping us later in the competition. I thought he was joking. His team-mates were Sarah Ulmer and Paul Leitch, so he had a hot team. I told him, 'Come on, man, you guys are cyclists. You're gonna kill us!' I attacked that hill climb the same way I had my rowing races and went hard right from the start. Partway up the hill, I glanced back. I couldn't believe it; there was no one in sight. I'd assumed the cyclists would win. But because it was such a steep hill and we were on mountain bikes, for some reason I was able to beat them.

It was the same in the Queen Street mile. By rights, it should have been an easy win for the runners. Top-distance runners are weedy little dudes with no upper-body strength, and they'd struggled in events that required power. This was their big chance. Rick and I had expected to get third and fourth behind John Campbell and Rex Wilson, who were two of the country's best marathon runners. Somehow, in the last 100 metres I managed to find a bit extra and got past them all. To be fair, the distance fell far short of what they were used to, but there was a lot of pressure to win events featuring your own discipline. To make matters worse for the runners, we beat them again in a race at Alexandra Park, where two team members pulled the third in a sulky around the horse-racing track.

Rick Wells

The runners were real grumpy about that one. They were well aware of the importance of winning their own event and it didn't help their mood that we were dressed in pink as we ran past them. Triathletes are known for their skimpy racing clothing, so Paul MacDonald decided that, as the show ponies of sport, our team colour would be pink. We thought that it was funny as hell. I roomed with Hamish and that's where I got to know him better. He was full of enthusiasm and keen to rip into everything, whereas I was more laid back. We were like the young and the old bull.

I seemed to be able to do well at anything that didn't involve pure power, and could muster more intensity than most of the others. I focused on trying to win, even if it was something I hadn't done before. Some of the guys would take off from the start, all guts and glory, then they'd blow up and sometimes barely be able to move. The mud run was a killer. The mud sucked you down and drained the strength from your legs. Some people literally had to crawl. The secret was to stay on your feet and keep moving. If you stopped, you were dead.

We had so many laughs during the show, but I don't know whether the Sheraton found it as amusing when we trooped mud and grime through the foyer and lounges after a day of filming. Not all the humour was for family consumption. One of the funniest moments — not mentioning any names — arose from a conversation about the loneliness of the international athlete. One of the boys piped up, 'Oh, it's not so bad. You can give yourself a blowjob,' and proceeded to demonstrate right there in the foyer. Thankfully, he kept his shorts on.

Another memorable moment happened at the army base in Waiouru. We had to abseil off a dam into the water below, then swim to a canoe and paddle off. We were kept waiting at the top of this big drop until the cameras were ready. I hate heights and was getting more terrified as each minute passed, but I wasn't half as scared as the guy next to me. Zinzan was a bit hysterical, yelling, 'Get me a glove, get me a glove.' The idea was to abseil as fast as you could by letting the rope speed through your hand, and I guess he was worried about rope burn. I was pretty cocky then, but not cocky enough to tell an All Black legend not to be such a pussy.

When we finally got the signal to go, Bruce Kendall (the Olympic champion boardsailor) let the rope go and fell like a stone — until his rope got twisted. When I caught up with him, halfway down, he was hanging upside down. Bruce was a really good guy: the nuttiest, most intense, fun dude you'll ever meet.

It was an education being with these people. Because there were so many well-known faces, our bus would be met by autograph hunters whenever we rolled into a town. It was a bit like being in a rock band. I was still an unknown, but it gave me the chance to see what life was like for some of the guys, particularly the rugby players.

In the final standings, the triathletes did well. 'Carter stood out on *Clash* not only for his distinctive curly blond hair, piercing blue eyes and wiry bod, but for the fact that he often left the rest of New Zealand's elite sports people for dead as he dashed out in front down the "Queen Street Mile" or kayaked like a beaver around Rangitoto,' wrote *North & South* magazine. 'Though the triathlon team finished second and third respectively in the 1994 and 1995 series, Carter was the star, the fittest of the fit. It was abundantly clear he was an athlete's athlete.'

We featured prominently on television each week and because I had a few wins (the mud run and the Sky Tower stair climb too) I suddenly had a public profile. Being recognised is a weird experience and takes some getting used to. I'd be out somewhere and notice people looking at me. I'm hopeless at remembering names and faces, so I'd be wracking my brain to try and work out if I knew them. People would say we'd met at some event or other and I'd have no recollection of it at all.

It was embarrassing and sometimes I'd be tempted to bluff it and pretend I knew them. John Walker described the experience well when he said that people look at you as though you're a ghost. You're a familiar figure to them because of television, and suddenly you're standing right next to them. They can hardly believe it, while you're wondering what all the fuss is about.

I was 22 then, and I can imagine that that level of public recognition could be difficult to cope with if it came suddenly, to a young rugby player for instance. But it also has its value. *Clash of the Codes* helped me along the way to becoming a professional athlete because having a profile made me more marketable. As people learned who I was, they also seemed to understand more about my sport. I was no longer asked whether I was a triathlon, or the especially embarrassing, 'Do you do triathletes?'

Around this time, a guy by the name of Roger Mortimer knocked on my door. I didn't know Roger but it turned out he had been a year behind me at Auckland Grammar. He had a marketing qualification, competed in triathlons himself and was trying to make a career in sports marketing. He was low-key, quietly spoken and not the type to make ridiculous promises about what he could do. I liked that. He's a guy who values deeds above words. He told me that he had some ideas that he'd like to try, in return for a small cut if any paid off.

Although I'd had no career other than sport, until then I hadn't thought much about how I might make a decent living from it. My passion was in striving to be the best. As long as I had enough money to travel, train and race, that was enough for me. I guess I can say that this was the season I became a professional athlete. Through the group of Australians I had trained with in France, I was invited to become part of a squad sponsored by the running shoe and sports apparel company New Balance. It was the first of its kind in triathlon and was run out of Japan, so we were required to do a couple of races there. Instead of having to rely on prize money to survive, I got enough from New Balance to cover the cost of my season. Any money I won became the icing on the cake.

I'd had good advice from my coach, Jack Ralston, who had worked with me since my school days. I met Jack because I was in Grammar's cross-country team and sometimes trained with another guy in the team, Andrew Peskett. One weekend I went on a long run with Andrew that started from his coach's house. That coach was Jack Ralston. I was 13 at the time and Jack would be involved with my training for the next 16 years. His background was in running, but he was one of the first coaches to adapt his methods for triathletes, and later trained several of the code's brightest talents.

Jack and I decided to take a different approach from triathletes on the international circuit, who'd chase the money from event to event. They would try to extend their peak fitness for long periods, travelling constantly, and often to races that in the overall scheme of things weren't that important. Consequently, many of them would be flat for the big races, such as the world championships, at the end of the season. Jack taught me to aim for prestige events and we set my training with those in mind. It meant contesting some races when I was below my peak fitness, but it was the right strategy. Jack and I always had a plan to win the big one.

Our marketing plan back then was to train damn hard, win a bloody big race, and then receive offers. If you could win a world championship (triathlon was not yet an Olympic sport) the earnings would come through endorsements and so on.

Jack was involved with Nike for a lot of the time we were together, but marketing me wasn't really part of our relationship. We were coach and athlete, so there was no problem when Roger offered to be my manager. Manager may be too formal a description for that first year. He'd go off and do his thing; I'd go off and do mine. Sometimes we might not catch up for a month. We were learning as we went. I was learning about being a professional athlete in a developing sport, and Roger was figuring out what was entailed in the fledgling business of sports management.

One of the first endorsements that Roger landed for me was with the makers of Rexona, the men's deodorant. Triathlons and sweat — yep, Roger was on to it. Rexona and I were a good fit, and so are Roger and I. I remember when he rang to tell me about the deal. It was around Christmas and I was on holiday at Mt Maunganui. I had to get on a plane back to Auckland, meet the Rexona people for lunch and sign the deal. I flew back to the Mount thinking, 'This is rock-star material, man'.

This was about the time that the movie *Jerry Maguire*, starring Tom Cruise as the slick manager of a rising American football star, came out. Everyone thought sports agents were kick-arse dudes who rolled around in $6000 suits with a cellphone stuck to their ear. Roger got a laugh out of that; he knew it was all hard work. One out of 10 potential deals might come off if you were lucky, and there were probably a hundred others Roger tried that I never knew about. He never expected much. Triathlon wasn't awash with money and it certainly didn't have the profile of rugby. It was more his passion than a business.

It wasn't long before it became much more than a business partnership and it's lasted 13 years now. There have been ups and downs, but he's become one of my closest friends. In fact, it was Roger I phoned first after crossing the line at the Athens Olympics.

Roger Mortimer

I'd always had a passion for sport. I did a marketing degree but wasn't interested in the traditional avenues, peddling soft drinks and toilet rolls. Grant McCurrach was a chartered accountant in town who represented Matthew Ridge, Va'aiga Tuigamala and Craig Innes. I went to work with him and that got me started.

Marketing sports people has changed dramatically. Back then, you'd phone marketing departments about sponsorships and they'd put you through to donations. Companies thought of it as charity, and it bears no comparison to the huge corporate response to Hamish after he won in Athens.

Triathlon is my passion and Hamish was New Zealand's top performer. That year, 1994, turned out to be quite significant for me, because Gary Ulmer, Sarah's father, approached me about managing her too.

I told Hamish I had some ideas for sponsorships. I can't remember now what they were or whether any of them came off. We were a couple of greenhorns. I'm six months younger than Hamish; it was his second year as a full-time triathlete and my first as a manager. We were both trying to find our way.

Back then rugby was amateur. I represented John Timu, who switched that year from rugby with Otago to rugby league with the Sydney team Canterbury Bankstown. The next year rugby went professional and opportunities for managers opened up. I managed a lot of rugby and rugby league players — people like Greg Alexander, who was captain of the Warriors, Dennis Betts, a British international who played for the Warriors, brothers Zinzan and Robin Brooke, Walter Little, Frank Bunce, Isitolo Maaka and Olo Brown. It was a lot of fun. They were good guys who'd had normal jobs and knew what it was like to have a bad day at work. That generation passed and by 2000 I'd had enough of rugby. But I still work with Hamish and Sarah.

It was difficult finding sponsors for Hamish in the early years. It didn't help that triathlon was a new sport that wasn't well understood. But there was good prize money at international level; he was winning or getting second in World Cup races right from the get-go. With the New Balance-Cannondale team sponsorship, he was able to be self-sufficient.

As the autumn of 1994 slid towards winter, I headed for France, rejoining Sutton and his band of Aussies at Alpe d'Huez. It didn't seem nearly as daunting this time. Experience is everything, I guess. It helped, too, that our accommodation was much bigger and nicer than the grotty little rooms we'd shared the first year.

Alpe d'Huez is perhaps the most famous climb to feature in the Tour de France. The route of the tour changes each year and towns pay big money to host a stage start or finish. This year Alpe d'Huez was on the itinerary. Stage 16 began in Valreas and finished down the road from our place.

By the time the riders got to the climb of Alpe d'Huez they'd raced about 100 miles (160 km). The Alpe itself has 21 switchback bends, numbered in reverse order, rising up to the town, 1860 m above sea level, close to the Italian border. It's about an hour's drive from Grenoble — depending on the quality of your rental car! The climb has gained such status because it's so abrupt and, in parts, so brutal. The average gradient is 7.9 per cent but it's as much as 14 per cent in parts.

The history of Alpe d'Huez in the tour dates back to 1952, when the Tour's organiser at the time, Jacques Goddet, searched for the most demanding *parcours* possible. Georges Rajon — one of just three hoteliers on top of what was then a rocky, pot-holed road — and two other businessmen offered £2100 (around US$3500) to Goddet to finish one of the stages up there. Organisers thought the idea ridiculous but were sufficiently intrigued to send the Tour's assistant commissioner, Elie Wermelinger, to take a look. He went in winter and needed snow chains to get to the top. At the time, the town of Alpe d'Huez was largely undeveloped, with not a ski lift or chalet in sight. Nonetheless, Wermelinger wrote a favourable report and the rest is history.

The first to win on the Alpe was Fausto Coppi. His Italian fans loved him. They referred to him as Il Campionissimo (the champion of champions). More than 40 years later, my Aussie companions and I saw Roberto Conti become the second Italian to win on the mountain. I'm not an aficionado but we got right into it and would watch the Tour on television in the afternoons after returning from training. A New Zealander, Steve Swart, was riding that year as part of the American Motorola team with Lance Armstrong. Swart made it to Paris, but Armstrong, who was riding his second Tour, didn't finish.

Each day the crowds would begin to gather on the mountain in cars, campervans and on bikes to mark out their spots on the side of the road. By the time the peleton arrived, there would be literally hundreds and hundreds of thousands of people there. The Tour really is a travelling circus, full of character and characters, and the fans are just as colourful.

We had some fun, too. Instead of writing the names of competitors across the road, as fans traditionally do, we painted our own names in huge letters. I'd be scanning the television coverage for the riders to pass over the piece of road where I'd painted 'Allez Carter!'

We also painted a big syringe on the tarmac, and got a bit of stick from fans about that. Road cycling had a reputation for drug use at the time, although not nearly as bad as now. It was still four years before the Festina car driven by team masseuse Willie Voet, with his boot full of doping products, was stopped by border police. Half of the top 10 overall finishers that year were later caught up in doping scandals. Marco Pantani, the flamboyant climber whose nickname was Il Pirato (The Pirate), was third and won the Tour in 1998. He was later busted twice for doping and died of a cocaine overdose in 2004.

I rode Alpe d'Huez in training plenty of times and even when you are relatively fresh it's huge. It demands respect when you're descending too, as I was to find out.

My training and racing were going well. I was consistently placing in the top three, usually behind Brad 'the Croc' Beven. He lived in Northern Queensland, crocodile country, and I think he got his nickname for that rather than from water being his natural habitat, although that was certainly true. In fact, he was one of the best cyclists and runners in the sport too. He had the complete package.

The 1993 World Championships in Manchester, where I was third and the Croc was fourth, turned out to be the last time I was to beat him for quite a while. For a long period he seemed to win every race he entered and I always seemed to be chasing him. I guess that made me the crocodile hunter. I think his consistency helped me to learn to be consistent too. I won in New Caledonia in May, claimed my second World Cup victory in June in Switzerland, and was second and third in World Cup races in the United States in early August. I was happy with my progress. Lying third in the world circuit rankings, I felt I was steadily developing as an athlete and was looking forward to the 1994 World Championships in Wellington, now only three months away.

Whenever we rolled out on a training ride from Alpe d'Huez, we'd first descend the 21 switchbacks to the valley below. Every time we'd say, 'Okay guys, we'll take it easy or else someone's going to get killed.' Then one rider would nudge the pace along a bit, then someone else, and it would get quicker and quicker, and before long we'd be bombing our way down the mountain. It was ridiculous.

The cool thing was you could always beat a car down, no matter who was driving. On one particular day, I was racing Ben Bright. He was in the rental, driving like a maniac to try to beat me. I was on my bike and in front of him going through switchback 18, with the bike laid over at a very steep angle, when my front tyre hit a small rock. It flicked the wheel out from under me. Everything happened so quickly that I was still holding the handlebars when I hit the ground. My knuckles hit first, then my shoulder. I rolled across the road into the barrier that stops you plummeting over the edge.

By the time Ben got to me, I was up, unsteadily, to my feet. I guess I was in shock. I was thinking, 'Oh man, that wasn't good'. Initially, I was most conscious of the pain from the grazes, but I soon realised that something was wrong with my shoulder. I could hear it crunching when I tried to move it. Then Ben told me that I looked really pale. Suddenly, a wave of nausea washed over me and I said, 'I've got to sit down.' That's when my shoulder really started to hurt.

I'd broken my collarbone. It was my first crash and the first time

I had ever broken a bone. Two days later I was on a plane back to New Zealand. I thought that was it as far as the world championships in Wellington went. I was quite down about it because my best performances had been overseas and I wanted to show the New Zealand public what I was capable of.

As it turned out, the collarbone was cracked rather than being a compound fracture, but it was still a potentially season-ending injury, depending on how quickly the bone healed and how much fitness was lost from not being able to train properly. But I didn't just sit on the couch and watch television. I ran in the pool, which eliminates jarring, and did some swimming workouts, mainly working my legs and with my arm on the damaged side strapped to my waist. After a while I could ride on a stationary trainer — but not on the road where every bump reverberates up your arms to your shoulders — and do a bit of running, also with that arm strapped to my body. It was far from ideal but I was desperate to race the world champs in Wellington.

I recovered enough to do a couple of warm-up races, one in Noosa where I went okay, all things considered, and one in Auckland, which I won. I was quoted in the media before the race as saying that everything had come back together pretty quickly and even suggesting that I was back to 100 per cent fitness. I don't know who I was kidding. I'd done only a handful of top-notch training sessions and there I was, thinking I was ready to take on the world.

I was still being tipped to win by some local media. And with Rick Wells racing, as a former world champion, you could say New Zealand was expectant. The race went right through the city and the number of people who turned out to watch was awesome, lining the streets around the waterfront. People wanted my autograph and this time I felt it was because I was a triathlete, rather than that bloke from *Clash of the Codes*. I'd been trying to keep things low-key, but eventually I got caught up in the hype.

I was aware of the high level of expectation and I think I knew subconsciously how unrealistic it was to think I could bluff my way through on such skimpy, post-crash preparation. A lot of family from Mum's side had come to watch. She was raised in Paraparaumu and cousins and aunts and uncles were coming to watch me for the first time. That sort of thing amounts to a bit of pressure and may have been a factor in a quite strange interview I gave. Looking back at it now, I think I was trying to water down local expectation, but it came across as though I didn't care what the public thought.

Under the headline, 'This One's For Me', I was quoted as saying: 'Everyone is looking to me to be the top contender but quite frankly I don't give a damn what people think. I've done the work and I'll be doing the racing. What everyone thinks and everyone wants is completely irrelevant. I want the race for my coach and for myself and that's about where it ends.'

It wasn't true, of course. Throughout my career I've loved nothing more than racing with the fern on my chest and doing my damnedest to do my country proud. What had happened was that my pressure valve had blown out because deep down I knew I wasn't ready.

Rick still had the ability to win that race but he'd been battling chronic fatigue and a string of sicknesses. I didn't have a great swim and by the time I got settled on the bike Spencer Smith was out of sight. He never got caught and won what was his third successive world title (one as a junior, the last two as a senior) with Brad Beven the only one to finish within a minute of him. I got a puncture about 5 km into the cycle. Rick, who wasn't feeling great, stopped and offered to give me his wheel. There was no point. You're not allowed to take assistance and I would have been disqualified if I'd placed. But, frankly, it wasn't going to be my day. Our women did better, with two in the top 10; Sarah Harrow winning bronze, and Jenny Rose crossing in seventh.

I took it hard. It was absolutely shattering. Instead of joining the partying that goes on after a world champs, I disappeared into my shell. Jack was there to remind me that it was just the beginning of my career, that there'd be other world championships I could win, but I was gutted. And all it had taken was a small rock on switchback 18 on the slopes of Alpe d'Huez.

LIFE IS BEAUTIFUL

Triathlon had a rapid rise to Olympic status but in so doing it threw a curve ball at the athletes. What it meant for me was that I had to reinvent myself if I wanted to make it at international level. In 1994, only five years after the ruling body, the International Triathlon Union (ITU) was founded, the IOC awarded the sport full medal status and announced that triathlon would make its debut at the 2000 summer games in Sydney.

Les McDonald, who has been the ITU's president since the union's inception, decided that triathlon had to become more television friendly and that the rule outlawing slipstreaming on the bike leg had to go. It wasn't a popular decision among the athletes at the time because it changed the whole nature of the race, but McDonald is an autocratic person who just put his head down and drove through the opposition.

I was against it initially, too, because making drafting legal neutered the bike leg, which was my strength. Under the new rule, a strong rider could bust his guts, towing along a bunch of guys in his slipstream and giving them a free ride, while ruining his own chance of outrunning them. Not surprisingly there were howls of protest.

It didn't help that not all athletes trusted the ITU, which had tried to foist some dodgy stuff onto us in the past. In 1997, for example, it presented athletes with a contract that required us not only to agree that our contract with the ITU took precedence over all other commitments — to our sponsors, managers, the national federation and so on — but also asked us to sign what was effectively a gagging order. This would have banned us from expressing any view critical of the sport or the ITU, and was accompanied by a threat to exclude us from World Cup races if we didn't sign. The union thought it had us over a barrel because we needed World Cup points to qualify for the Olympic Games, but there was such an outcry that the ITU backed down.

However, McDonald stuck to his guns over the change to legalise drafting. For some athletes, it was catastrophic. A few moved to long-distance events, such as Ironman races, where drafting remains banned; others stopped racing altogether. It also ended the dominance of Spencer Smith. He was a big guy with a lot of power, the sort who could ride easily in a big group at 40 kph or ride off the front by himself at 45 kph and still pull out a strong run. He was never a great runner, but if he had a lead of two minutes on his wheels, he could run well enough to stay clear. He had a simple but effective strategy: stay in touch during the swim, bike everyone's brains out, then hang on to the finish. It wasn't in his best interests to cruise along quietly on the bike, waiting for the run to decide the race. Smith was one who moved to longer distances, along with Cameron Brown and Australian star Greg Welch. The latter two excelled at the Ironman distance. I particularly missed having Welch around. He was a character, not one of your cocky Aussies, but a real affable entertainer always keen to spin a yarn.

The drafting issue triggered a lot of fighting and some major screaming matches. McDonald copped a lot of abuse but he did have a vision, and you have to give him credit for pretty much single-handedly getting triathlon into the Olympics.

In reality, drafting had become impossible to police over shorter distances where the field is more compact. Even in Ironman races, you would often see a line-up of athletes on the bike trying to get as close to the draft zone as possible without getting busted and having to serve a time penalty. I hated the bitching and moaning that went on after races about who was drafting. There'd be protests galore. Legalising it stopped all that, and after a couple of years, nobody complained any more. So it was a good move, although I didn't necessarily see it that way at the time.

Not only was I struggling to get my training right, I was struggling to get my attitude right. It took me a long time to learn to sit back and relax during the bike. I'd always be pushing up at the front, driving the race along. I thought my number was up because there were plenty of guys racing who were better runners. They'd hop off the bike with much fresher legs than when drafting was illegal and outrun me every time.

Gradually, I was forced to accept that the bike was no longer such a crucial element of triathlon. For a while I thought you could just cruise, but that proved to be wrong. The stronger cyclist you are, the less the ride takes out of you, and weaker cyclists are still made to pay when hills, wind and cornering make it tough. Winning breaks are still made during the bike leg. As the sport evolved, it tended to be held over multiple laps of a tight circuit instead of one big loop. The idea was to create a better spectacle, but it also made bike-handling skills more important and the ride harder, because there were more corners, each requiring braking and accelerating.

The change heralded a new tactical approach. The race was no longer a time trial. It didn't pay to just go flat out the whole way. You had to figure out how to manage your workload on the bike, and decide when it was wise to use your energy and when it was smart to be patient. It was about timing and balance again. Someone is always trying to break clear. Do you go with every attack, maybe get away in a break but start the run tired, or ignore attacks and save your energy for the run? The risk you take is that if a breakaway gains a couple of minutes, your race is gone. Either way, it's a gamble. If the leading group doesn't contain any known runners, the bunch is less motivated to work hard and chase the bolters down.

For a time, I decided not to go with any breakaways during the first half of the 40 km cycle. That meant I was watching attacks go off up the road knowing that any one of them could spell the end of my race. That's nerve-wracking, especially if it's a big race that's been the focus of your season. Often there'd be rows on the road. Runners tend not to contribute much on the bike, although there's an unwritten code that everyone in a breakaway does their share of the work. When that gets ignored, there can be screaming matches, although I don't recall any physical fights. We're all pretty skinny so they'd be pretty pathetic, handbags-at-high-noon sort of fights. Shane Reed, a Kiwi, had a reputation as a bit of a slacker. One year, he won in Noosa after not pulling his weight in the successful breakaway. He didn't gain any respect, but it's his race and he can do whatever he wants.

The move to draft-legal racing meant I had to change as a triathlete. I needed to be able to swim like a fish to stay in touch, but most of all I had to learn to run like a gazelle. I was solid, but had a long way to go to become what I call a real runner.

The first change I made was to virtually hang up my bike during the New Zealand summers — the off season for the international circuit. I ran and ran and did little cycling. As far as training went, I tried to forget I was a triathlete. I had to swim like a swimmer and run like a runner. To do that, I needed to train with the best from those two sports.

While my collarbone was mending, national swimming coach Mark Bone helped me with drills and later invited me to join his elite squad. That included Trent Bray, Guy Callahan and Nick Tongue, all phenomenal swimmers. That squad transformed me. Swimming became my mainstay and, with one or two exceptions, I came out of the water in the front pack from then on. The best swimmers are so smooth and fluid. I'd study them, watch their every move underwater and try to copy them. They had what swimmers call great 'feel' for the water. They catch so much water every time they put their hand in and, although they're flying along, it never looks strained.

Getting kicked in the head . . . whacking your arm into someone's shin . . . salt water down your gullet . . . feeling like you're going to drown . . . That's what a triathlon swim can be like if you get caught in the ruck at the start or around the first buoy, wrote journalist Margot Butcher in an article about me in *Metro* magazine. 'The most dramatic moment of a triathlon is not the last, but the first,' she wrote. 'From the air, it looks like a feeding frenzy of small black orca. A still sea suddenly boils with wildly slapping arms and legs, churning blue water into white.'

It can be bloody scary if you get caught in the rough stuff. You have to sprint out of the blocks because if you don't smack it for the first 200 metres and get out in front then you're gonna get thumped. I stopped worrying about that after joining Mark's squad. In fact, the second-best feeling in a triathlon became waiting for the starting gun to crack because I could just about count on being one of the first round the buoy.

I couldn't do the volume of training that Mark's 'pure' swimmers did and still have energy for running and cycling. Over time, through trial and error, we got the amount about right. It meant that I would sometimes get out of the pool early, which wasn't easy, because not finishing a session is bordering on sacrilege. Initially, I'd drive home from the pool feeling a bit down although I knew that that was how it had to be.

Mark Bone

Hamish had a broken collarbone when I met him and wasn't swimming. He was going out with Natasja Hilgeholt, who I was coaching, and would come down to the pool with her and mooch around. I told him not to be such a pussy. It's easy to play on injuries. I told him there were lots of things he could do. He needed to work on his kick; that would help his aerobic capacity and his big leg muscles, and would minimise the loss of overall condition from the injury. The leg muscles are so important in both cycling and running. They're the biggest muscles in the body and we can work them pretty hard in the water. He could also work on sculling, the small hand and wrist movements that help swimmers maintain their feel for the water.

I guess I was trying to create a rapport with Hamish and also let him know I was a bit of a tough bugger. I was national coach at the time, which was then a voluntary position, and I was employed by

Carter Collection

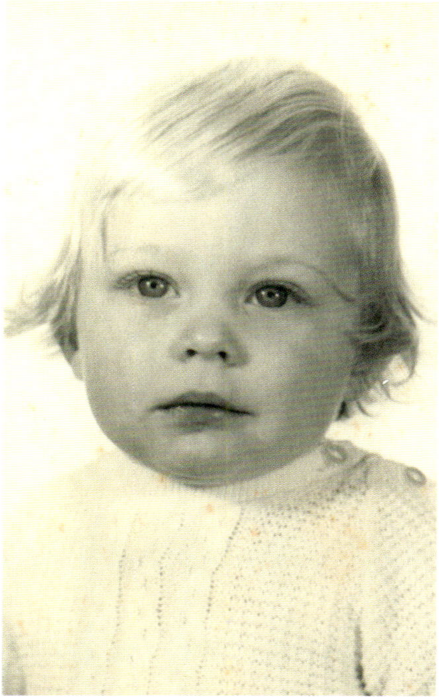

Carter Collection

ABOVE: Early days at Lucerne Road, Remuera, Auckland. From left: Tom, James, Doug and Cath, with me in front.

LEFT: One of the few baby photos of me, wearing a nice knitted jumper. There weren't many. Not surprising considering I was the youngest of five.

Carter Collection

1980, my ninth birthday, and probably around the time I had seen John Walker and had my dream.

Carter Collection

Tom pulling me in the rubbish bin — we didn't have many toys, so had to make do!

Carter Collection

And years later . . . this was the day after Phoebe was born (12 March 2004). Austin and I at a St Kent's school fundraising visit. It was also our wedding anniversary.

Carter Collection

An early attempt at a family photo. Dad always tried it on the cheap before deciding to spend $$$$s on a project. From left: Doug, Dad, Mum with me in front, James, Cath and Tom.

Carter Collection

Another attempt at a family photo taken around 1983, this time by a professional. That's me on the right.

Carter Collection

Mates on a surfing trip in 1987. From left: Matt, Thor, me and Dan.

Carter Collection

Auckland Grammar Eight win the Bay of Plenty Shield, 1989. That's me doing the honours.

Carter Collection

Clash of the Codes, about 1992, during competition against the Aussies. It was incredible to compete alongside people such as Ian Ferguson.

Carter Collection

Clash of the Codes triathlon team — Rick Wells, me and Sara Harrow talking to media.

Carter Collection

With my mum at the finish of the 1993 World Champs in Manchester, and an ever-present drug-testing chaperone.

Carter Collection

One of the first international events in Noumea where I joined Team Foster's for one race. It was a rare situation to have 'groupie' girls flown in to support the athletes.

Lester de Vere

Marisa and I stroll barefoot along Pauanui beach on our wedding day.

Carter Collection

2004: Austin and Phoebe waiting for dad to come home from the Olympics with a medal.

The family in 2004 — taken post-Olympics. That's why we all look so happy!

> a swimming club, but I was one of the few who thought we needed to embrace those from other aquatic sports — triathletes, surf swimmers, water polo players. I had triathletes in my squads and passionately enjoyed coaching them.
>
> Rick Wells had retired and there was no dominant swimmer on the triathlon circuit, so I thought there was room for someone to make an impression. Triathletes didn't understand the intricacies of training as a swimmer, how to break it down into what's needed to swim fast, and it wasn't going to happen for them if they just swam together. I was lucky to have some top swimmers in the squad for Hamish to learn from. Bray, Callahan and Tongue were all on the national team, all Commonwealth Games medallists and all part of a relay team that won gold at the world championships.
>
> Hamish had good conditioning from his rowing background. He was streetwise and he worked diligently on perfecting his stroke technique, but it was a struggle for him at first. I remember a training camp we had in Cambridge that nearly killed him, but the result was a massive advance in his swimming. He developed to the point where he could have led out of the water. That's until Andy Potts, a United States Olympic swimmer, came along. But Hamish was good enough to swim on his feet.

I was lucky that I naturally felt at home on a bike and had the necessary strength, thanks to rowing, to ride well, so I didn't need to clock up masses of miles. Eventually, I settled on a regime where I'd pick up my cycling about three months before a targeted event, but still only ride six hours a week. However, the improvement from training with Mark's top swimmers confirmed that I needed to do the same with my running.

Increasing my mileage was one thing, but I had to learn the essence of being a runner. That's when I began to pester Alan Bunce. I'd met him at *Clash of the Codes* where he was supporting Maree, his wife at the time. I rang him out of the blue and asked if I could join his training runs. Alan was a national road champion, a real talent for whom a big international future had been predicted before being dogged by injury. He had a reputation as a hard trainer and a tough competitor.

To run fast, my legs had to be fresh enough to get the most from my training runs. If you're tired from big cycling miles, you just plod along. Cycling crushes your ability to run fast, and rowing is worse. A rower running looks like an elephant thumping down the road. Having run at school gave me a big head start but I had to learn to move differently. Runners have a term to describe it: 'running in a bucket'. Triathletes don't run tall, their hips are down and they're flat on their feet, which means they're on the ground for a long time. Great runners run further forward on their feet, their hips are up and they stick their butt out, so they run taller and spend less time on the ground. If you have poor running technique, it's as if the ground is a barrier blocking your progress with each footfall, whereas runners tap themselves forward with each step.

Alan was nursing an injury and wasn't that keen to have a feisty young triathlete hanging around, but I was persistent. He relented so much so that I ended up living with him and Maree for a while. That association changed me as an athlete, because I was able to run with him and because it led me to Chris Pilone, who later became my main coach.

You don't become a good runner overnight. I was capable of running 10 km in 32 minutes fresh, but I needed to be able to pull that out when I was tired at the end of a triathlon. That sort of improvement doesn't come in weeks or months.

Alan Bunce

We started meeting up for some runs and I could see immediately that Hamish was a consummate professional. I didn't need to motivate him at all, it was more a case of just watching him and noting little technical points. He used to run like quite a few triathletes, as if he was still sitting on his bike seat, so I got him more upright and into some drills to improve technique.

I cut a minute from my 10 km run time in a year. Swimming and cycling remained important, too. If you're not in the front pack off the bike it doesn't matter how fast you run, you're not going to win. You need to be in that front group. With no ban on drafting, if you're not one of the best runners, you rarely win. The run is like the last card in your hand and you have to play it at the right time. How is everyone else going? Do I need to try to run the sprint out of them by pushing the pace a long way out? Or should I wait? The run is where any triathlon is won or lost.

I raced well in the season after my disappointment in Wellington, with four wins and a dozen other placings. The best result was winning a World Cup race in Auckland, where I dealt with the danger of Miles Stewart's fast sprint by attacking with 2 km to go. It was fantastic to win a big race in my hometown with family and friends watching. After Wellington, I couldn't let them down again. The only blight on the year was eating something dodgy in Mexico, which meant my 1995 World Championships was ruined by diarrhoea. I finished the race in Cancun, but was almost last.

The next year, 1996, was weird. I battled with chronic fatigue and got caught up in the political turmoil of a rebel circuit that was trying to challenge the ITU, coincidentally around the time of the Super League versus the ARL battle. It was called the International Triathlon Grand Prix (ITGP) and staged events that were very short, with each discipline often over multiple laps in an attempt to make the competition closer and more appealing for television. The people who backed it had money to spend and we were paid appearance money and put up in nice hotels. Everyone thought triathlon was stepping up to foot it with the tennis circuit. It didn't last, but they were cool times. For me, the appeal was that the ITGP attracted a lot of the top guys, such as Simon Lessing and Greg Welch, and I wanted to race the best. The crunch came when triathlon gained Olympic status under the control of the ITU, which threatened to ban athletes on the rebel circuit. The Olympics is the biggest deal of all and I was dreaming of winning it.

From 1997, I felt the changes I'd made and the work I'd put into my running had started to pay off. That season I was one of only two people to win twice on the international circuit. I finished fourth in the World Cup series, second at the world champs and ended the season as the second-ranked triathlete in the world. I was on my way.

That was the first year New Zealand Triathlon put together a structure for athletes competing internationally and secured some Sports Foundation money to use for an altitude camp. The first year it was in Albuquerque, New Mexico, then Flagstaff, Arizona, and then we shifted to Europe, to St Moritz in the Swiss Alps. Most of New Zealand's top triathletes used the camps. Mark Elliott, who became high-performance manager, instigated the programme. Mark had a background in multi-sport and a second placing in the Coast to Coast race across the South Island under his belt. He is also a physiotherapist, so he would do the massages, while his wife, Jude, helped in all sorts of ways. It was simple but effective stuff, and they made sure we had what we needed to put in top-quality training.

Mark and Jude had a Bedford truck called the Hippo because it was a total piece of shit. They toured Europe in it, stopping in winter to pick up jobs such as running ski chalets. In summer they'd take a break from their travels, park the Hippo in a paddock, and set up the altitude training camp for two or three months. It was brilliant, a home away from home. As well as a great location for training at altitude, those camps provided an umbrella of security and stability. There were certainly no frills — we were often three to a small room — but for me it was luxury because Mark and Jude made it all so easy. In the past, I'd have to spend February frantically phoning triathletes around the world to see what their plans were and to figure out who I could work in with to set up a mini-base from which to train and travel to races. Often two or three bases were needed because the races were in different parts of the world. If you tried to go from motel to motel and race to race, it would cost a fortune and you'd go insane. When my brother Doug lived in London, I'd often stay with him and Abbey for a couple of weeks at a time.

That first year (1997) when our camp was in Albuquerque, I was 13 seconds away from becoming world champion. I don't know if I should be happy about coming second but there were plenty of positives. I had one of the fastest runs, and for the first time got the better of two of the sport's best runners, Simon Lessing and the Croc, Brad Beven. It topped off a year that was good in more ways than one.

I trained really well in Albuquerque and went from there to a World Cup race in Cancun, Mexico, which I won just because I was so damned fit. Cancun wasn't normally a happy hunting ground for me because I'm not a great racer in super-hot conditions and it was about 40 degrees and 90 per cent humidity. It was so hot that there was no point going for a warm-up — I was sweating just standing still. The course was as flat as a pancake and that doesn't suit me either.

I didn't feel great at any time during the race. We pushed the pace the whole way on the bike and I found myself alone in the lead during the two-lap run. Your brain isn't the sharpest when you're racing, with your muscles demanding most of your oxygen, but I became more fuzzy than usual. I wasn't hallucinating, but as I came to the end of the first lap I was convinced it was the finish. I was so relieved it was almost over.

Then, to my horror, about 50 metres from the finish there was a cone in the middle of the road and an official was waving me around it. It was a massive struggle to get my head around the fact that I had another 5 km to run, and my state of distress wasn't helped by the knowledge that the Soviet athletes Dmitriy Gaag and Volodymyr Polikarpenko were running me down.

I made it, but only just. In the last kilometre I felt as if my body was shutting down. My vision was packing up. It was like this darkness was closing in, narrowing my sphere of vision, until it was like looking down a slim shaft. I was slowing, unsure whether I'd make it, and that got worse close to the finish as the crowd of shouting people beside the road thickened and blocked any breeze. It was oppressive, like being wrapped in a warm blanket.

I've felt brilliant in races and been beaten; this was one where I felt very average and won. I was in such good shape that I was able to fake my way through. It was a great race for New Zealand, with Jamie Hunt and Paul Amey coming home fourth and fifth. It showed how good Mark Elliott was at creating a good training environment. It was my first World Cup win since Auckland two years earlier.

Two weeks later I won again in Sydney, making it back-to-back World Cup wins, which doesn't happen often. But what was magical about the Sydney race was how effortless it seemed. I had grovelled in Cancun, but in Sydney I felt as though I was floating. It was one of the few days in my career where everything clicked. During the bike, there were times when I was dropping the pack without even trying, and when we came off the bike, I ran away from the opposition even though it felt like I was cruising. I couldn't get over it. No matter how hard I pushed myself, I couldn't make it hurt. Even with 2 km of the 10 km run to go — a stage of the triathlon when you are usually only just holding it together — I still wasn't hurting. It was ridiculous. I've never dominated an international race like that and it wasn't a weak field. All the top Australians were there. Welch was second, a minute behind, and Miles Stewart was third. Both were former world champions. The Australians had been all the talk before the race; it was meant to be their show.

'Underdog Carter upstages favourites' was the headline in the *New Zealand Herald* the next morning. Kiwis got a laugh when I said, 'I love the smell of barbecued Kangaroo.' It was good to deal to them in their own backyard and nice to be the first foreigner to win a World Cup race in Sydney. It didn't hurt, either, that top officials from the Sports Foundation were in the crowd. And to top it off, this was the first race held on what would be the course for the 2000 Olympics.

I could see my Olympic destiny. I believed that was what my life was about; and with this win, I could see it coming to fruition. I'd felt untouchable and it had seemed so natural, as though I was a puppet and that some powerful force was at work to make the fairytale come true.

I was flying, and in just two weeks I would be in Perth racing for the title of world champion. I was walking on air, but not just because of my form. There was a new girl in my life.

My relationship with Natasja Hilgeholt had come to an end by the training camp in Albuquerque. We'd been together about three years. She was from Christchurch and raced internationally too. It was great to have a girlfriend to travel with and share life on the road. We'd be in Spain one weekend, Italy the next, then off to race in Japan and America. Although all the travelling can be hard, it was a pretty amazing lifestyle for people in their twenties. Natasja had a couple of top-10 finishes in World Cup races and was one of those athletes who was always on the fringe of breaking through to the next level. It was a pretty incredible time, but the reality was that we weren't ideally suited and the relationship came to a grinding halt in 1997 when I started to get to know Marisa.

Marisa was a good swimmer before becoming a triathlete. She was in the New Zealand team for the 1993 World Championships in Manchester and also for Wellington the next year, so I knew who she was, although we didn't get to know each other until four years later. It's funny to look at the 1993 team photo because it appears as if we're looking across at each other, whereas everyone else is looking at the camera.

I had seen her around the triathlon traps and also in town when she was wearing her business clothes. She looked a bit of a corporate destroyer, going out selling million-dollar deals. She has a no-nonsense approach and a strong personality. I immediately liked that about her. It's an attractive quality but can also be a bit intimidating. She doesn't stuff around.

She was working in marketing for Mojo, an advertising agency that had the Qantas account, when she contacted me about an idea she'd had about putting together a triathlon team the airline might want to sponsor. We discussed it over coffee and when I went overseas we emailed back and forth, business-like at first, then more friendly. It was at a stage when you could say a lot more in an email than you might over the phone or in person.

I just about blew any chance of a relationship right at the beginning. We'd been emailing for about a month but hadn't even talked on the phone. A friend, Jason Windhager, invited me on a kayaking trip in the Marlborough Sounds that he was planning for the Christmas holidays. His partner was going and I told him I'd broken up with Natasja but to put me down for two spots because I was emailing this girl and hoped she'd work out. I was sitting at the table in Albuquerque typing the email to Jason and pushed send. Two seconds later I realised that I'd sent it to Marisa by mistake. I panicked and yanked the phone jack out of my computer in an attempt to stop it in cyberspace, but when I checked my 'Sent' folder, there it was.

Oh man. The language I'd used in the email was typical of the way you talk to a best mate. 'Yo, dude, I've got this chick on the go who could be keen. Put me down for two and if it doesn't work out, I'll find somebody else to take.' I sat there for 10 minutes staring at the screen. I thought I'd blown it. I looked like a stalker, some psycho who just assumed Marisa would fall at my feet. She was very diplomatic about it. She wrote back, 'I don't think this email was for me.' She came on the trip and by Christmas we were definitely an item.

Because of the time difference it would be 2 p.m. in Albuquerque when Marisa got into work in the morning in Auckland to clear her emails. I'd do my training and would then sit by the computer waiting for two o'clock. I'd then be emailing more or less until I went to bed. The emails were just friendly, maybe a little flirty. It was a difficult period because Natasja and I had been going out for a long time and she'd been a big part of my life. Marisa knew Natasja, and I told Marisa that I had sort of ended it. Instead of Marisa saying, 'Good, because I think we get on well,' she was telling me to think it through.

I got back to Auckland after winning in Cancun and had been home about half an hour before I rang her and suggested we get lunch. I think she was a bit surprised that I called so soon. If you're playing it cool I guess you'd wait a couple of days, but I thought, 'Bugger this, I've got to see what she's like'. We clicked instantly, although that lunch was a bit weird. I remember her holding the knife and fork and they were shaking, really shaking. She hardly ate a bite and her voice was shaky. I thought she was either a nutcase or a little nervous, which was funny for someone as assertive as she is. She called later and admitted she'd been nervous. I asked why and she said, 'Well, you're Hamish Carter.' I was like, 'So?'

It was that exciting new relationship time and I was fizzing when I went off to Sydney and won that World Cup race. When you win, people come up congratulating you and it's a buzz to hang around, go to the function and soak it up, but I couldn't wait to see Marisa. I got a flight back to Auckland that evening. It got in quite late and Marisa was there to meet me. We'd only been out a few times and I was going to get her to drop me home but she said, 'Look, why don't you stay at my place.'

I hesitated, wondering if it was too soon, whether it was going to get a bit crazy. But then, typical Marisa, she said, 'I've already made the decision, you're staying.' I enjoyed her decisiveness then and I still do.

Consequently, I went to the world champs in the best of moods. I was ranked number two in the world and I was in love. I guess there was pressure, but I don't remember feeling it. I was looking forward to the race. By the end of the bike there was a lead group of 10 which included most of the big names including, significantly for me, the Englishman Simon Lessing and Brad Beven. I'd raced those guys my whole career and hadn't been able to get the better of them, so consequently still had a bit of a mental block about beating them.

Chris McCormack, the New Zealand-born Sydneysider, bolted out of transition and put 60 metres on us. He'd recently broken up with his girlfriend and had a real fire in his belly. I still wasn't too concerned because he had a reputation for attacking too early and dying. Besides, I felt I was in the right position tracking Lessing, who was second on the road and only 10 metres ahead of Brad and me. I'd got into my rhythm and was holding a little in reserve when, after about 3 km, I dropped Brad. I couldn't believe it. I'd chased the guy in so many races during the past few years that it almost came as a shock. I couldn't claim victory over him in the World Cup race in Sydney because he'd crashed on the bike.

I ran up to Simon. I was a little awestuck to be tracking this guy who'd won the world title three times. I thought that this was the race right here, between the two of us. Halfway through the run, McCormack had an 18-second lead but I still thought he'd gone out too hard, too fast. Then, slowly, it began to dawn on me that Macka wasn't fading and that maybe Simon wasn't able to haul him in. I'd have to have a crack myself. With 2 km to go I squeezed the accelerator and Lessing slipped behind. I had a few moments of disbelief because these guys were my nemesis and I was beating them — not because I'd got away from them on the bike but because I was out-running them.

I quickly had to remind myself that the race was up the road and it was make or break. One kilometre to go and the gap was just seven seconds. He was right there, dangling in front of me. I could almost touch him. A former runner, McCormack was an Australian representative at junior level and on this day he refused to blow up. Still, I thought I had him. I thought I was going to become world champion. We were running towards an Australian crowd that thickened as the finish drew closer. He races on emotion and I saw the cheers lift him at the same time as I felt my body groan. At the line, I'd missed becoming world champion by 13 seconds.

I'd put in a very good race, had a breakthrough in beating Lessing and Beven, but more than anything I felt gutted that I'd allowed their reputations to limit my performance. I probably lost 15 or 20 seconds by holding back. I'd run with Beven thinking that it was a case of holding on to him for as long as I could before he dropped me. Then, instead of striking out after McCormack, I ran with Simon for 4 km waiting for him to run up to McCormack. It was a harsh lesson. The world championship had been there for me and I'd let it slip away. Macka had pulled one out of the bag.

Even so, it was a return to the top of the sport for me, so I went out and celebrated that night. There were a lot of positives. Tony Veitch had come over with a TVNZ crew to do a story. I did interviews with Tony, and a camera crew followed me around in the lead-up to the race. Mum and Dad had flown over to watch. Even though I came second, I had a clarity about my sport, a real belief that I was capable of beating anyone and that I could do it with a camera crew in my face. I was young enough and arrogant enough to think that I'd figured out the problems I had had coping with the pressure at the worlds in Wellington three years earlier. The momentum towards the Sydney Olympics began with this result, both in terms of my own expectation and also the beginning of the pre-Olympic media hype. I started to figure in articles predicting who would win New Zealand's first medal in Sydney.

I felt like I'd nailed the year. Jack Ralston was still my main coach but I had new input from Chris Pilone and Mark Bone, plus the Alan Bunce factor. I'd hit peak form at just the right time.

The next year, 1998, was just as good. New Zealand's triathlon academy high-altitude camp was in St Moritz, 1700 m up in the

Swiss Alps. Again, I won two World Cup races and was fifth or better in eight of the nine races I entered in the series. The exception was in Cancun, where I didn't handle the 40-degree heat.

My running continued to improve. An example of that involved Dmitriy Gaag, the archetypal silent Russian, although the fact that he doesn't speak English might have something to do with that perception. He's from Kazakhstan and was one of the toughest guys to beat in the late 1990s, despite looking like he'd just gargled a bottle of vodka. Gaag out-sprinted me down the finishing chute of a World Cup race in Japan and we duelled again a couple of weeks later in Hungary. Gaag put 100 metres on me straight out of transition. He was just flying as he ran past me. But I knuckled down and slowly clawed him back, then overtook him and stayed in front to win the race. I was becoming a bit of a runner . . . but not quite good enough, as it turned out.

The world championships that year were in Lausanne, Switzerland. I'd taken the lead in the World Cup points table in May and went into the race as the world number one-ranked athlete, a ranking I held until the Sydney Olympics. The result was a bit of a shock, not because Lessing won but because Paul Amey beat me. It was the first time in a major race that I was challenged and beaten by a fellow Kiwi. That was hard to get my head around. Paul was in the second group on the bike, along with Miles Stewart, but their group caught us and about 30 athletes went into the transition together. Lessing led for most of the run with Paul, the Swiss Jean-Christoph Guinchard, and myself chasing. I had problems. I'd recently started to use a sports drink (I used to drink water or water mixed with Ribena or Raro) and my stomach felt bloated and I was having trouble breathing properly.

Guinchard dropped off, but Stewart, who is renowned for his finishing kick, caught us with a couple of kilometres to go. We couldn't afford to wait for a sprint. About 1500 metres from the finish, Paul accelerated and I struggled to respond. I finished fourth, 12 seconds behind Paul. I was right there to congratulate him. If someone beats you fair and square, you have to accept it.

I'd not thought of Paul as a threat, partly because he doesn't put it together very often in races and also because you don't want to give your opposition the idea that you think they can beat you. It's an attitude. You have to be a little bit arrogant and back yourself. But I wasn't surprised that he pulled it off. I'm surprised to this day that he hasn't done it again. He trains harder and faster than probably anyone I know. The quality he can produce is up there with anyone in the world, so I've never understood why he wasn't a contender more often. He never won a World Cup race, but on that day in Lausanne, he showed his true talent.

Once again at the world champs it was a case of 'close but no cigar' for me. I finished the season off well with a win in Auckland and a second in Noosa, and had the consolation of winning the World Cup series. It was my first international title and, as Jack told the *Herald*, it was something I'd worked towards for five years. 'He's served his apprenticeship and now he's the most consistent athlete of the year,' said Jack. 'But there's still a lot of room for improvement. His running is nowhere near what it can be. He may be the best in the world right now, but he knows you're not judged until you've won a world championship or an Olympic gold medal. That's the next step.'

MR INDESTRUCTIBLE

A newspaper reporter nicknamed me 'Mr Consistency' and then a magazine profile appeared under the headline 'Get Carter'. It meant there was a perception that I was getting close. It meant that although I didn't always win, anyone with aspirations to win had to beat me first. Over two-and-a-half years, I'd missed the top five just once in 15 World Cup races, and had won five of them. My world ranking rose from 25th in 1996 to second the next year, then to number one from 1998 pretty much through to the 2000 Olympics.

Like the kid's game, King of the Castle, you're constantly fending off attempts to knock you from your perch. Consistency had kept me there for a long time and had kept the money coming in, but sometimes your strength can also be your weakness. The most consistent athlete often doesn't claim the biggest prize. If you're always doing well, at what point do you get fired up enough to do something phenomenal? Sometimes you need to go through a slump to get to the start line of a major race angry enough and aggressive enough to tear it apart.

Training and racing around the world made for a good lifestyle and

I counted some good mates among my rivals. In the lead-up to a race, you're pretty much stuck in your hotel. You can't tramp around like a tourist all day or it ruins your race — as I'd discovered on a couple of occasions. You try to stay off your feet as much as possible.

Sometimes a group of us might go to a movie, but we'd be more likely to rent one in the hotel. And although it was great to visit new cities, in reality I didn't get to see much of them. I hung out a lot with Chris 'Hilly' Hill, an Aussie who's an awesome guy and a hell of a lot of fun. I missed him when he retired. A quirky little dude who wore glasses when he wasn't racing, he was nicknamed 'The Professor'. He didn't look like an athlete, but when he was on form, he was one of the hardest to beat. In 1998, we had a great battle in a World Cup race in Auckland. He bolted away at the start of the run and I don't think I would have pegged him back if it wasn't for the hometown crowd.

A junior world champion, Chris won silver as a senior. But he's also a very talented guy who never ceased to surprise with his range of abilities. I thought I knew all about him after a couple of years on the circuit together, then he'd hop onto a piano at a party somewhere and be brilliant. When I visited his house I commented on all these great paintings hung on the walls. 'Oh yeah,' Chris said, 'I painted those.'

I loved kicking back with him. One time in a flash hotel overlooking the Sydney Opera House, we'd put the phones in our rooms on speaker and keep the line open all day, chatting as though we were sharing the room. I'd buy him shandies for a joke when we were in Australia, because if you order a shandy or quiche over there somebody is going to kill you.

One hard-case experience we had was in Minnesota. That's one weird town. It had become a destination for the world's top triathletes when a Humvee-driving local multi-millionaire, Bahram Akradi, decided to promote his fitness business, Lifetime Fitness, by staging a race with such a big winner's purse that it would attract the best male and female competitors in the world. The women get a start, calculated on the difference between male and female winning times, and the first across the line wins the big cheque — which is now up to US$150,000. We'd done the race, packed our bikes and were ready to head out when three stretch limousines pull up and three gorgeous girls jump out. Everyone's going, 'Holy shit, this is more like it!' because on the ITU circuit we get treated like chopped liver. Here we got VIP treatment; the limos took us wherever we wanted to go. At one nightclub we were waved past a long queue outside and seated in a reserved area where we could hang out with the 'beautiful people', separated from the hoi polloi by glass walls. It was Paris Hilton material.

In winter, Minnesota gets as cold as 20-below and is prone to blizzards for months on end, so when summer arrives, people go nuts. Everyone's out partying. Girls grab guys off the streets. I'd never seen anything like it. When we walked back to our limousine from the nightclub, we noticed that it was rocking. Hello, we thought, what's going on here? We couldn't see through the tinted windows, so Hilly and I clambered up and peered through the sunroof. Inside we could make out two bodies and lots of naked flesh. The same thing was happening in the limo parked behind — it was the drivers with some girls. We were thinking, 'Oh my God, what is it with this town?' It was classic.

Big nights out are rare, though. You might have one or two a year, after a big event like the worlds perhaps, because you can't afford to get hammered too often. You've got to be your own machine and get yourself up for a race, even if you're feeling crap, because you don't travel with a support crew. It's you versus the world. If your life is a shambles, you don't last long on the World Cup circuit. That's why triathletes are like single-scullers; they're focused and disciplined, but there are plenty of flamboyant characters when the gin and tonic comes out — and it generally only takes one glass.

That said, triathletes aren't like conservative single-scullers when it comes to fashion. The gear we wear is probably the most frightening element of the sport and I've got to plead guilty to being a tragic when it comes to fashion. Over the years I've worn some diabolical clobber. New Balance had a horrible purple team uniform and Nike put out a turquoise number that clashed dramatically with my garish green bike. Possibly the loudest item I ever wore was a pair of bike shorts that made a Crunchie Bar wrapper look conservative. I did look a bit of a gimp.

For racing, you need something tight enough not to slow you down during the swim but comfortable enough for the bike and run. I swam in Speedos or bike shorts with a singlet tucked in that I could pull up as I ran out of the water — until the IOC made a rule that you had to cover your torso during the swim. That's when the one-piece racing suit came into vogue. For a while I raced with white zinc on my nose and got grief over that. I looked like an Australian cricketer running around in his underpants.

In the early days, most of the Aussies raced in Speedos, or 'budgie smugglers' as they called them. Sarah Ulmer used to love giving me stick about our kit. She reckoned guys should be arrested for running around in that sort of get-up. So did my training mates. Most sports have their traditional gear, such as the conservative shorts and singlets worn by runners. I'd turn up in a dazzlingly bright pair of pants and they'd say, 'Mate, you can't run with us dressed like that!' Swimmers would be horrified if you came to training in anything but Speedos, but then the cyclists weren't happy if you wore skimpy Speedos on the bike.

Some of the girls looked great, though, and although I didn't make a habit of looking closely at the guys, a few made an effort. Some of the Europeans, in particular, looked like they'd been chiselled out of granite and had stylish racing kit. At times it could be intimidating, turning up to race them straight out of a New Zealand winter, pasty white and a bit chubby. Gradually, I came to accept that I had no fashion sense and that it wasn't the area in which to make my mark.

My big aim for 1999 was the world championships in Montreal in September. We'd planned to sacrifice a bit of form early in the season to have me at my peak for that race. I'd placed second and fourth the previous two years, and thought that making a mistake with my drink had cost me my chance in the last one (I'd reverted to plain water). I felt that I'd learnt to handle pressure and had shown that when I won a World Cup race in front of an expectant Auckland crowd in 1998 after being beaten into third the year before. I was 27 and should have been at my physical peak. I felt as though I had everything dialled in. Instead, it turned out to be the start of my Olympic rot.

I placed fourth in two World Cup races and second at the Oceania Games behind Greg Bennett in early-season races, then headed back to the New Zealand Triathlon base in St Moritz for six weeks of altitude training. This time I took Alan Bunce with me to make sure that I had the best possible running training. I covered his expenses and his mortgage for a couple of months and he did all of my running sessions with me. It cost a small fortune, but I thought it was necessary. I'd never trained as hard on my running as I did during those weeks. The problem, although I didn't know it at the time, was that it was probably too hard; I destroyed myself.

When we came down from the altitude camp, I won a World Cup race in Hungary, only a month before the world championships. Even though I hadn't felt great, I was encouraged because it was my first race in three months, I hadn't tapered my training to freshen up for it, and most of the top contenders were in the field. But I got killed at the world champs in Montreal. I led out of the swim, but the bike and run was raced on a Formula One track where you're always in sight, and for the only time in my career, virtually the whole field came together on the bike. Sixty-odd of us charged off the bike and into what became purely a running race. Gaag won from Lessing and Stewart. I finished 11th — 45 seconds behind the winner.

Two key factors ruled against me: I had trained too hard and the pancake-flat course didn't suit. I later came to realise that I was best on courses with a few hills. As I got older I was becoming stronger, but not necessarily faster.

After the race, Marisa and I spent a week in New York on a delayed honeymoon. We'd got married in March at my parents' bach beside the beach at Pauanui, but only had a few days there together before I went overseas on the circuit and she returned to work at TVNZ. The two of us hadn't mucked around. We'd bought a house in Mt Eden about six months into our relationship and were married within 18 months of that first shaky-handed lunch date.

Marisa

Hamish did the house hunting. I was working and he liked filling his days after training looking at houses. We liked this place instantly. It had everything we wanted, including a deck and a view. I was a little hesitant because we hadn't been together long and I'd just come out of a long relationship. I told him I didn't want us to live together unless he was thinking long term. Later I found that he wasn't thinking much at all. It was a place to store his stuff so he wouldn't have to pack up every year when he went overseas.

Anyway, we signed the deal, he flew off on the World Cup circuit, and I hired a truck and two men and moved in. The two men became a standing joke between us because we weren't married then. I spent the winter there with wooden floors, no curtains and no couches. When the phone rang, it was like an echo chamber. We got the house sorted when we got married . . . it's adorned with wedding presents.

I think Mum was happy with how things worked out. It's funny, but before Hame and I got together she had seen him interviewed on television and said to Dad, 'Why doesn't Marisa go out with someone like him?'

I was frustrated by how the world championships had panned out but there were plenty of pluses for me going into Olympic year: my hard training would hold me in good stead, I'd been consistent enough to retain the number-one world ranking, and I'd still been the first Kiwi home at the worlds.

Jack and I decided that I needed to concentrate on running over the New Zealand summer. The Olympics was the only race that counted in 2000 and we wanted to do one long, steady build-up, peaking for the Games in September rather than for qualifying races early in the season and then having to peak a second time. I thought that my leading world ranking and being the top New Zealander for the past six years would be enough for my selection to be rubber-stamped. I discussed this with one of the selectors, Graham Park, and came away with the impression that my place in the team was guaranteed — although they still wanted me to do the selection races. The selection criteria that had been talked about was a top-10 placing in World Cup races and finishing in the top 15 at the worlds. Well, I'd done that several times during 1999.

Consequently, I hardly touched my bike over summer. Then the bombshell fell. Two weeks before the first trial race, which was on the

Sydney Olympic course, I was told that, like everyone else, I had to qualify. There'd been a misunderstanding and we were both at fault. I had wanted Graham to bend the rules and his response had been, 'You're good enough; don't worry about selection.' He was trying to be helpful, telling me what I wanted to hear. Or maybe I heard what I wanted to hear.

I'd faked my way through to win a World Cup race in Hawaii, having got away with a soft bike leg. That wasn't going to happen in Sydney, where the bike course required a lot of strength. I was knackered by the end of the ride and ran accordingly. Ben Bright was the bolter. He finished fifth — the first Kiwi home — and under a revised selection criteria gained automatic selection. He'd pulled out a freak race. After retiring for a while, he had little in the way of international results, whereas my consistency counted for nothing. One bad race and I was back to square one.

'We can't rely on past glories,' Park told the media. 'It comes down to form now. Hamish has to accept the fact that he's not our No 1 man at the moment. We'd love him to be there because he's produced the goods in the past, but he knows that when it comes down to the big ones, you've got to perform. He has two weeks ahead of him and a lot of soul-searching . . . the pressure has come on from the other guys and it's a wake-up call he's got to handle.'

I was totally distraught and leaned heavily on Marisa and Jack. I felt that I'd climbed my mountain by rising to the top of the sport, and that the one higher peak I needed to conquer was the Olympics. Nobody told me that qualifying would be an even higher mountain. There I was, like a dog in the gutter, fighting for a place with everyone else.

My final chance to prove myself was at the world championships in Perth. But that was only two weeks away. How in the hell was I going to transform my biking in such a short time? There's not a lot you can do in such a short period. My training had been geared towards a race still five months away, yet somehow I had to beat half a dozen guys who'd trained exclusively for these qualifying races.

I couldn't sleep the night after the Sydney race and things only got worse. The next day, all the athletes with a chance of qualifying were made to sit through a long briefing on what to expect at the

Olympics. They even measured us all for uniforms. It was ridiculous and piled on unnecessary pressure when, at that point, only one of us had bloody qualified. Everything was stacked against me, yet everyone seemed to take it for granted that I would qualify. VISA had put together a pictorial book of New Zealand Olympic legends — including the likes of John Walker and Mark Todd — and had also put me in it!

On the weekend that I was home, between the races in Sydney and Perth, Marisa and I went away with a group of friends to Rotorua. It helped me chill out. I did a lot of riding, we had some laughs, and for a few days I managed not to think constantly about my predicament. I faced a simple equation. One spot had gone and a second spot would go to the most consistent performer over the two trials. I'd finished 32nd in Sydney, so that wasn't going to be me. My only chance was to get a high placing at the world championships and be first Kiwi home.

Marisa

Our kitten, Couscous, symbolised that stressful year. First of all, she meowed all night, as kittens tend to do when you first get them home. Then we lost her for several hours and then she set the house alarm off in the middle of the night. We'd had the alarm sensors adjusted so that she wasn't supposed to be able to set them off and I'd wanted to test them before Hamish went overseas. That set Hamish off, too: 'The effing cat's going back!' I even rang the pet store; that's how serious it was. But they weren't keen to take her back, so Couscous stayed. We're glad she did. She's become a bit of a media star, featuring in Purina petfood ads with Hamish, and more than earns her keep.

The world champs coincided with Graham Park's birthday and I decided we should get him a strip-a-gram. Paul Amey and I had a lot of fun touring Perth's strip clubs, choosing the stripper. Some establishments had menus, complete with pictures, and at one the girls paraded for us, although they kept their clothes on. In deference to the younger team members, we didn't book the 'full Monty'.

Graham took it in the spirit intended but inevitably a complaint was made to Triathlon New Zealand and I had to apologise. I didn't care. For me, it was a perfect diversion from the stress.

At the race, I swam well and made the breakaway group on the bike. Strong riders Craig Walton and Olivier Marceau were there, but no stand-out runners. It was the sort of group I could hope to win from if I were at my best, but I was barely hanging on. It was wet and slippery. I misjudged a corner and found myself 10 metres adrift; I had to get back into the shelter of the group's slipstream quickly or I'd be a goner. A group that's working well together develops a momentum of its own, like a train that has worked up to speed. That's where cycling expressions such as 'getting on the wheel' come from, because getting into a group like that is a bit like boarding a train. I hauled myself back up to them but the effort nearly killed me. The other riders had noticed that I'd slipped off the back and had sped up in an attempt to shake me off for good.

I started the run with such tired legs that I was hanging on for grim death the whole 10 km. The race had been delayed two hours to avoid photographs of the finish being ruined by the setting sun, so we were racing into the gloom of dusk. I was in trouble physically and my vision was packing up. That, combined with the failing light, meant that for the last hundred metres or so I was running virtually blind. Somehow I made it across the finishing line. The next thing I was conscious of was an IV drip that was being put into my arm. Jack was there. 'Did I do it?' I asked him.

Jack Ralston

It was a muck-up from the beginning. This was the first time these selectors had selected Olympians and there were conflicts of interest. John Hellemans, one of the selectors, was also coaching athletes vying for places in the team. I was wrongly led to understand that Hamish only had to do a solid performance at a trial and he was in.

His race at the worlds was one of his greatest. So many variables went wrong, and not just during the lead-up. There was a stuff-up over the distance; the athletes were told the run was three laps when it was four. Chris McCormack was in the lead on the third lap. I was

> yahooing in the finishing chute, thinking we'd got second, when to my horror an official jumped out onto the road with a sign telling the athletes that they had another lap to go. It cost McCormack a spot in Australia's Olympic team. He let it affect him and faded to 15th place. This is where Hamish showed his determination. He hung in and hung in. He wasn't going to let that Olympic spot go.
>
> As he was approaching the finish, I saw his knees go loose and almost buckle. I thought, 'Oh my God, the boy's in trouble'. He collapsed on the ramp as he crossed the line. He was out to it. They wrapped him in tinfoil and put him on a stretcher. When he came to, he said to me, 'Did I make it? Am I in the team?' I didn't know for sure, but I said, 'Yes, yes you are.' He smiled and grabbed my hand. A bit later, in the recovery tent, he nodded at the drip in his vein and said, 'Plug that into a can of beer, will you?'

I'm more proud of that race in Perth than just about any other. Hawaii Ironman great Mark Allen once said that a great athlete is not someone who wins a race, but someone who performs even when they're having a bad race. For me, Perth was that race. I shouldn't have been able to get in the top 10; I simply wasn't fit enough. I had to draw on every ounce of natural ability and fight every step of the way.

Luck is such an extraordinary thing. Jamie Hunt, who'd sat in the chasing bunch, came to the front of the group late in the ride and crashed on the final corner, bringing Craig Watson down with him. Had that not happened, they would most likely have run me down and put me out of the team. Both were great runners, as Craig showed at the world champs the following year when he did the fastest run time on his way to the bronze medal, and Jamie showed again in this race. He'd closed to 14 seconds behind me by the finish and might have become world champion but for his crash. The spill cost him a minute and he finished 48 seconds behind the winner, Marceau.

I wonder how both of our futures might have panned out had that crash not happened. Jamie would have gone to the Sydney Olympics instead of me. Who knows what that would have meant for each of us in the long term. Careers and dreams turn on such things. Within a year, Jamie had retired. We'd spent time together during his four years on the World Cup circuit. You live life from race to race, often relying on beating friends and colleagues to earn enough prize money to continue. It's intense when you're single, let alone when you're responsible for a wife and young child, as Jamie was. His full potential wasn't realised, even though he was twice world junior duathlon champion, and picked up a second and a third in World Cup races.

I didn't enjoy racing him — or Amey for that matter — because I knew what they were capable of. They could be devastating. There are a lot of athletes in triathlon like that. Part of it is to do with the difficulty of perfecting three quite different sports. An athlete might be phenomenal in one or two of the disciplines, another might be brilliant in training. The hardest thing about triathlon is getting all the variables spot on for race day.

Qualifying against the odds had a powerful effect on me. It re-ignited my sense of destiny, which came back even stronger. I could see the path leading me to the top of the podium in Sydney. The hardship I went through to qualify, Jamie and Craig crashing . . . it was as though some higher power was testing me, but at the same time ensuring that I'd be in Sydney to win. I started to believe this rubbish again.

It's fair to say that I've never suffered from a lack of confidence. Referring to my 'unabashed personality', journalist Margot Butcher wrote in 1999 that I debunked one of the oldest traditions of New Zealand sport: I didn't pretend to be the underdog. As I told her then, my philosophy was that you're not doing yourself any favours pretending that a win is some sort of bonus.

It was around this time that I called in on my manager Roger and gave him, of all people, a real rark-up. It's a day I'm embarrassed about and that I put down to youthful naïvety. I'd got carried away with myself.

My profile was high and people would periodically tell me that I should be landing $100,000 sponsorship deals and making a million bucks a year. I guess it turned my head. Rog is unassuming and understated, and those are absolutely among his strengths. But there I was, thinking that I was pushing myself, pushing my coaches and that we all needed to be dialled in, including Rog. I was oblivious to the masses of work he put in that didn't turn up trumps, the pitches that didn't get a bite, the deals that fell over. He didn't bother me with that sort of detail. It wasn't as though we didn't have good sponsors leading into the Olympics. We did. But I had this idea that I needed to push him to be like the movie character Jerry Maguire and make sure he was busting his balls for me. I went to see him and crudely laid it on the table. 'Dude,' I said, 'I'm not feeling the love here. Are you out there for me? Are you pushing hard enough? Where are all my contracts?' I guess I thought that when you go to the Olympics, you could add a zero to your bottom line. Rog, in typical style, took it on the chin. But years later I'd remember it and cringe. What a wanker I was.

Roger Mortimer

Our relationship could have gone two ways that day. To be honest, I was pretty tempted to grab his file and say, 'Here, take it. I don't need this. I'm not in it to be treated like that.' He basically said that he was world number one and that I should be doing a lot more for him, but in much harsher words. I think I mumbled something along the lines that I was absolutely committed. I'm a very poor salesman when it comes to what I do and never really communicated that to him. I got the impression that I probably wasn't too far away from being fired. It cut me deeply because you're not in this for money — not when you look back on it as an hourly rate. But you get other things out of it, like that night he won in Athens. The richest man in the world can't buy that experience.

I still don't know why I didn't walk away. For a long time afterwards, I sometimes wished that I had. That was in 1999. Then came Sydney and then 2001; three pretty hard years. I've no doubt that Hamish was totally carried away with his own press. Part of me is pleased that he didn't win in Sydney. If he had, I don't think he would be such a good person now. I think he would have been a poor Olympic champion. That sounds harsh, but he wasn't ready. In 2004 there were no athletes in Athens more deserving of their gold medals than Hamish Carter and Hicham El Guerrouj, who won the 1500 metres and 5000 metres double after taking a tumble at the 1996 Olympics and being pipped in 2000.

My own hype and self-belief after I qualified may have rubbed off on the others in my little crew. We didn't stop to question whether we could do it. We were leading the game but, really, we had no idea what we were doing. Jack had been working overseas for Nike and then in Wellington for the New Zealand Rugby Union. I'd been running with Chris Pilone's athletes and, consequently, Chris was having more and more input into my training. I guess that Jack was concerned about who was calling the shots and he said, 'You can't have coaching by committee. It's either my way or we flag it.' Fair enough. Jack needed to back himself.

Roger and I were young guys and still growing into our roles. Roger's involvement then was very much just with sponsors. Something had to give. I wanted both Jack and Chris as part of my programme, and then there was Rog and my swim coach, Mark Bone. Jack was trying to retain overall control and it was a bit like being caught with two girlfriends. I had to make a call. Although Chris had done some great work with me, I opted to stick with Jack. He'd coached me for so long. Maybe loyalty clouded my judgement, but Jack had been such a major part of everything I had achieved. He would have seen it as someone else moving in on his turf and I couldn't do that to him. I thought Jack was the guy I wanted to go to the Olympics with. It came to a head at a meeting at Strawberry Alarm Clock cafe in Parnell. Jack chaired it and the tone was, 'Right, we're here to win gold.'

Chris Pilone

I'd helped Hamish informally from about 1997, while Jack Ralston was overseas. Towards the end of 1999 I had a few misgivings about the plan heading into Olympic year, both regarding Hamish's training and how Triathlon New Zealand was planning to approach the Games. It was triathlon's first time in the Olympics and, as I've since learned, it's a very hard atmosphere to deal with. I thought they were a bit arrogant and I didn't feel right about it, so I tactfully withdrew.

Roger Mortimer

The meeting at the cafe was indicative of the time. The whole environment around Hamish was bad. It was all 'Team Carter: Let's

Get Ready To Win Gold In 2000'. Ralston was, in effect, the manager. It was a strange meeting and a strange time. Chris and I didn't talk about it until three years later, but it had an impact on me. I remember getting in my car afterwards and thinking, 'Man, this isn't good'. But then I thought, 'Jack knows what he's doing. If this is what it takes to win a gold medal, then this is what we do.'

I think Hamish suffered from the inexperience of the people around him; none more so than myself. I'd been through an Olympic campaign with Sarah [Ulmer] at Atlanta, but she was very young, the expectations on her weren't too high and I wasn't closely involved. Sydney was the first Olympics where I was part of trying to create the right environment. And I think Sydney was an environment where Hamish was arrogant.

I think Jack Ralston created an atmosphere of arrogance. We were a green team. We went in thinking that we had a chance when we had no idea what we were up against. I don't think Simon Whitfield had a 'dream team' behind him, but he benefited from the fact that nobody knew who he was. He was ranked about 30th in the world. The Canadian media weren't even there when Canada won its only gold medal. They had to rush across Sydney from the softball. Simon's the nicest guy in the world and it was well deserved, but things went his way. He had a low-key, low-stress lead-in to the race. Ours was anything but.

Jack Ralston

I wanted to get clarity about the arrangements. My group of runners had gone different ways and the Sunday group sessions weren't happening. Hamish was running with Chris and his guys. Roger was sitting on the fringes giving advice, Mark Bone was having his input, too, and if you put Chris in as another influence it could result in confusion. I might have been telling Hamish he could win it off the bike, while Chris was telling him he could win it on the run, and Mark was saying something else. I told them, 'Let's all get together and talk it through.' Chris was an absolute professional about it. He stepped back, but he still allowed Hamish to run with him. Hamish had the option at that stage; he could have gone with Chris.

I was 13, rowing and running at Auckland Grammar when I first met Jack. He coached one of the school cross-country runners and I tagged along with him on one of the long runs that left from Jack's place on the North Shore on a Sunday morning. Jack is a flamboyant character and a natural storyteller. After those runs, we'd listen to him talk about sport for hours. He's a people person and I guess that's why he loved coaching. He can be inspiring. Those characteristics must run in the family because his brother [media personality] Bill Ralston seems to share those traits — although I can't imagine Bill out pounding the pavements.

Jack was a good athlete and came on the runs with us. He could run downhill particularly quickly. Just when we thought he was miles behind, he'd swoop down one of the big hills on the loop we did and come flying past. Jack was a force in coaching. He shaped a lot of the careers of young athletes, including mine. I was 21 when I started in triathlon. I told Jack that I wanted to do it full time and become world class. We sat down and tried to figure out how. Jack's training theories were based on Arthur Lydiard's methods, but he'd also coached and managed New Zealand athletics teams in the '80s and '90s and picked up knowledge from the coaching systems of the Russians, East Germans and Italians. He instilled in me the discipline of sticking to our plan of targeting no more than two or three races a year, and to structure my training accordingly.

Jack Ralston

Early on, you wouldn't have said Hamish was great at anything. There were others more talented in the school cross-country team. When North Shore Bays' top two runners were away with the national team, Hamish was hauled in for the club relay champs. He ran the uphill lap over the Kaimai Ranges and lost two minutes to the Owairaka team member. He was pretty depressed at that but we'd seeded our runners right and the team came through to win. So Hamish won a national running title before he won one as a triathlete, but you wouldn't have picked him then as an outstanding athlete.

What he did have was a unique fire. I call it 'fire in the belly'. He'd do all that he could to improve. You never had to motivate him because

> he had such a powerful desire. In fact, you had to be careful not to kill him with too much hard work when he was young. Cameron Brown was leader of the pack among the triathletes in my group when Hamish came along. But Hamish didn't consider himself inferior to anyone. If he was able to train with them, he couldn't see any reason why he couldn't beat them. He never put barriers in his way. That attitude remained with him as he progressed. It's a distinctive trait in most athletes I've coached, but I have never seen it as burning as in Hamish. He had this belief — a vision — that he was going to be an Olympian. He'd talk about how John Walker inspired him. If a Kiwi like Walker could do it, why couldn't he? That was his attitude. I had a replica of Walker's gold medal, set in a Perspex dome, that I'd bought at a charity function. I gave it to Hamish and said, 'Hold on to that until you win your own.'

I'd kept to my usual regime of training at altitude in St Moritz and followed that with second place at a World Cup race in Lausanne one month before the Olympics. My last lead-up race became a non-event due to a puncture in the transition area, so Jack and I organised a training race at Gulf Harbour, north of Auckland, and called in some good athletes to chase me along. I was riding away from top cyclist Paul Leitch and running away from Paul Hamlyn, who four years later represented New Zealand in the 1500 metres at the Athens Olympics. My fitness was where it needed to be and I'd survived the selection curve ball.

Marisa, her parents, Mum, Dad, my sister and brothers and a lot of friends were making the trip to Sydney. It was all about to happen for me.

DAMAGED GOODS

Triathlon was the first event of the Sydney Olympics. The women raced on the first day of competition, the morning after the opening ceremony, and the men's race was the following day. There was no way we could stay in the athletes' village without being totally disrupted by the excitement and chaos of the opening, so Triathlon New Zealand had arranged a house for us in Botany Bay, on the other side of the city, away from all the hype. But getting agreement from Les Mills, the Chef de Mission of the Games team, wasn't straightforward.

Kayaker Paul MacDonald had warned me that it would be an absolute circus. He had previously won five Olympic medals, so he knew what he was talking about. I figured I could avoid getting caught up in all the excitement by jealously controlling my environment. My plan was to fly into Sydney, go to the house at Botany Bay and stay there as much as I could until it was time to race. I wanted to block out the whole Olympic vibe until I arrived at the race venue. That's what I believed I needed to do to give myself the best chance to win. I thought I'd be able to handle the pressure of the race itself — it would be like the world champs, only bigger.

As it turned out, forces beyond my control meant that my plan began to crumble almost immediately. The triathlon team was told we had to stay in the village for at least one night. I'd already got off on the wrong foot with the New Zealand management at our first meeting, when I'd basically told them that I was going to win a medal so they should just give me what I needed — no village, no team stuff — and leave me alone to do my own thing. Les Mills more or less told me that my individual performance wasn't what counted; the team was more important.

I reacted badly to that and decided it was them or me. From that moment on, I bucked against everything they wanted me to do. The Olympics are an endless list of requirements and restrictions, and every single one of them bugged me. Marisa had been working at TVNZ and the officials had got the idea that a film crew was going to interview me in the village. Against the rules, I was told. Then the triathletes were dumped with the worst accommodation, a windowless duplex box stuck on the end of someone else's quarters. I jumped to the conclusion that it had been done deliberately to piss us off and I wasn't impressed. Now that I understand the logistics of the Olympics, I realise that it was perfectly reasonable to put us there as we were only staying one night.

I was guilty of getting carried away with my own self-worth, no question about it, but Mills and his officials didn't make it any easier for me. The way I saw it, Mills had created an ethos where the athletes weren't to get in the way of the Olympics. My experience four years later in Athens, where Dave Currie was Chef de Mission, was the complete opposite. Currie would go along with anything, within reason, if it helped the athlete to achieve his or her best performance on the day. Helping the athletes win medals was his top priority. I think the whole triathlon team thought Les Mills was negatively affecting our races, but I took it more personally because I was driving that attitude in the group.

Once we were at the Botany Bay house, I still couldn't relax. There were too many people coming and going that shouldn't have been there: coaches and various hangers-on. A nutritionist even came over to try to tell us what to eat. It was a bit late for that sort of thing. I was furious. This was *my* Olympics and as far as I was concerned, all these people were ruining it. I needed peace. All I'd wanted at the house were the four athletes (Craig Watson, Ben Bright, Evelyn Williamson and me), the coaches and team physiotherapist Mark Elliott and his wife Jude, who we were entirely comfortable with as a result of the altitude camps they ran.

The final straw, as far as the triathletes' relationship with management went, came the following day when we were late for the New Zealand team photo. The photo had to be shot again to include us and everyone else was kept waiting while we took our places. Mills' officials shot us dirty looks that said, 'Who the hell do you lot think you are?'

They were right. We'd assured them that we would be on time for team functions and right off the bat we were late for the first one.

If you have an ego, the Olympics changes you. I became a bit aggressive and adopted a 'stuff you' attitude, and I think Jack caught the bug. You want your coach to support you, but we were both in a foreign environment and didn't know what we were dealing with. I always thought that being part of the team would be the coolest thing, but I felt alienated, as though I was some arrogant punk who'd been blacklisted. I was in a vicious circle, worrying not just about the race but about what the New Zealand team thought of me. I was losing energy virtually by the hour and had no idea what to do.

Jack Ralston

> The management was naïve and the whole environment was strained. Les Mills and the NZOC had come up with this 'one team, one dream' image and no one was to break that. It was their whole philosophy. Les wasn't completely dictatorial, but I think the people around him ran it that way.

I'd been refusing media interviews but relented on one occasion. The reporter asked what it was like to be one of the country's best hopes of a gold medal. That brought the pressure of public expectation flooding back. In my desperation to control everything, I'd managed to shut it out. Before I'd left New Zealand, my name had figured in every article or report discussing medal prospects, and some of my sponsors had even told me what they had planned for 'when' not 'if' I won a gold medal.

Being reminded of those expectations spooked me. I felt freaked and completely off target. Jack told reporters on the eve of the race that the triathletes were like 'skittish horses' and that Carter was the most skittish of all.

Jack Ralston

I believe that I was wrong in not being more forceful with Hamish in impressing on him that he could win the race on the bike. He was never convinced that he could. He came out of the water with a half-minute gap. There was Simon Lessing (England), Craig Walton (Australia), Hamish, and one other who faded quickly. All three were strong riders. The Aussie coach and the English coach were sitting near me and they said, 'Jack, there's the medals sorted out.' That's how convincing it looked.

Then, on the screen by the grandstand in the finish area, I saw Lessing ease up. It was early in the ride and he was planning to sit in behind the others to save his strength as he was the fastest runner. The others were talking together and decided it wasn't on. I didn't think the bunch would get organised enough to chase them down; they'd want to save their running legs and three riders can get around the tight turns quicker than the pack.

A lot of things were going through Hamish's head. He was worried that Lessing was going to leech off them, and I'd never quite convinced him that he could get away on the bike. We'd had several arguments about it, although I'd never call them arguments. With Hamish, it was always really straight talking.

In the end, I wasn't insistent enough and we probably weren't experienced enough at that top level to really have a crack on the bike. Walton might have been caught on the run but the other two were good enough to stay away. Hamish would never have been satisfied with a silver medal behind Lessing, whereas I tend to think if you get silver you should be bloody proud.

Deep down, I knew when I dived in the water that I wasn't going to have a good day. The emotional stress leading up to the race had overwhelmed me. But at the Olympics that's not something you're willing to acknowledge. I was still in the hunt at the end of the bike, in the main bunch with Simon Whitfield, who ran through to win. But any hope I retained was extinguished the moment I began to run. There was nothing left in my legs.

I couldn't watch the medal ceremony; it was just too painful. I wanted to get as far away as possible. I felt such a fool; my dream had been so wrong. Everything I lived for had come crashing down around me. I knew that the experience would change me but it was too much to face right then, so I pushed it away.

Marisa flew home to Auckland to return to work a couple of days later and for the next 10 days I threw myself into supporting the other Kiwis. For the first time I actually felt part of the New Zealand team. Mills' officials seemed to appreciate the support I gave the others and some may even have changed their view of me. I guess I'd become a decent person again. In a way, I felt I owed the New Zealand team something because I'd let them down.

Inside, I was eaten up; not an hour would pass without my mind drifting back to the race. When sculler Rob Waddell won a gold medal, I busted through security and ran a New Zealand flag over to him. It was great to see another Olympic triumph for my old sport and I was rapt for him but in my heart I thought, 'God, I'm such a loser. The high point of my Olympics is someone else's race.'

When I wasn't wallowing in self-pity, I still managed to have a bit of fun. I'd worked bloody hard to make it to the Olympics and was determined to get something out of it. I went out most nights and got blotto at the closing ceremony, thanks to a bottle of vodka that Mandy Smith, the hockey player, sneaked in.

At the closing ceremony, the athletes were penned under the stands for ages waiting for our moment to swarm into the centre of the stadium. It was hot, cramped, and there was a last-day-at-school atmosphere. Chantal Brunner, the long jumper, climbed up on to one of those metal trays that carry the wiring and other utilities, and took off her tracksuit top to cool down. That prompted a chorus of

'Get your gear off' and she entered into the spirit, peeling off another layer. There were lots of laughs like that.

Marisa

He partied every night for two weeks straight and would ring me at work each morning in his hung-over state. I was over it after a week and told him it was nice that he'd been partying with the basketball girls, or whoever, but he didn't need to tell me all about it every day.

His race was the result of that whole stressful year. Hamish doesn't remember it as being so stressful, but I think it's his mind blocking out what was a really bad time. There was the selection debacle and then the stress around the actual Olympics. Considering that we hadn't been married long, it wasn't a particularly happy year.

Clive Carter

It was so painful to watch him go through the experience of Sydney. I think Pat even said to Hamish, 'This [triathlon] has to stop, we can't take any more.' We were in the grandstand, Doug and Abbey had flown from London. It was the first time we were all watching as a family. We'd thought it was all on.

I think the mental approach was wrong. I don't want to put it all on Jack, but he kept telling Hamish that he was going to win. It was a good lesson; there are too many good competitors out there to take anything as a given.

There was no dodging the gloom once I got home. New Zealand had won only four medals and the hatchets were swinging. I copped it big time. According to Sports Foundation chief Chris Ineson, the Kiwi team had lacked the necessary mental toughness and the work ethic to achieve on the world stage. I was one of a handful singled out as a waste of money. Carter had 'a real crap race', said Ineson.

I reckon he was smarting over the 'picking winners' policy that he oversaw. When it didn't come off, the athletes got dumped on. But one of the great things about sport is its unpredictability. Favourites get beaten.

I'd got to know Chris well over the years and he'd really been a guy in my corner. The foundation had been one of my biggest supporters but I guess when the shit hit the fan he had to explain. I tried not to take the comments personally because I don't think they were meant that way.

I had failed to deliver, but the criticism came across as though I was a greedy, overpaid athlete who hadn't tried. Triathlon had received nearly $1,000,000 in foundation funding during the three years prior to Sydney and the way it was reported made it sound as if I'd personally pocketed it all. I'd received some good grants from the Sports Foundation during those years but not much more than $50,000 in total, and very little of that in the Olympic year.

It wasn't as though there'd been no return on that money. I'd topped the world rankings for all of those years, had won a World Cup series and had finished no more than 45 seconds behind the winner (in a race that takes the best part of two hours) in the four world champs prior to the Games.

What Chris Ineson didn't mention was that triathlon's funding had been slashed for the lead-up to the Games because we didn't have a good world champs in 1999 — falling from $550,000 in the 1999–2000 season to just $86,000 for the 2000-01 season that included the Games. That meant that the altitude camp at St Moritz was just about deserted because the second-tier athletes couldn't afford to go. I'd been given a grant of $7000 that I put toward my costs for the two-month camp, including fares. To try to do an Olympic campaign on $7000 is just insane. You just can't do it. Ben Bright and Craig Watson had been given only about $2000 each. I called and begged the Sports Foundation to give them more money so that we could all go to St Mortiz. They increased it to $3000. All three of us went there but it was far from ideal because there were no training hacks for us to work with. Four years later, at my training camp for the Athens Olympics, I had Liam Scopes and Clark Ellice dedicating themselves to my cause. What a difference those guys made; they were literally worth their weight in gold.

But the result is the result and I don't want to use that as an excuse. Craig did best of the three of us, finishing 16th; I was next, ten places further back; and Ben was 38th.

Roger Mortimer

I thought Chris Ineson was inept. He backed Hamish's build-up to Sydney; then when things didn't go the way we all hoped he took a very public swipe at Hamish, and Hamish was hurt by it. But he didn't let on just how hurt, because it's not the Kiwi guy thing to do. I thought Hamish was courageous in the way that he dealt with it and I respect him hugely for having the fortitude to try again. Most people would have walked away.

Mark Bone

It was a flop, but that doesn't mean he didn't try. Hamish never throws in the towel. Unless there's a puncture or crash, he always finishes. He's a very proud guy. The moment you start not finishing races, is the moment you show softness. He's never done that. People didn't appreciate that although he didn't have a great race, he still went to the finish line, and afterwards he fronted to everybody.

I travelled back to Auckland with the Games team. There were a lot of reporters at the airport and Kay Gregory from breakfast television asked me straight up if I felt that I'd let the country down. For about half a second I wanted to punch her but then I realised that she was right. That was exactly how I felt. I had to own up to my own sense of failure. It wasn't a PR strategy; it was something I needed to do for myself. Yes, I wanted to win. Yes, I failed, and yes, I did feel I'd let my country down. I knew that if I couldn't accept that, I'd never be able to move on. I'd been sent to represent my country, like a soldier sent to war, and I hadn't got the job done.

If I couldn't explain the result, I could describe how it felt: 'I felt crappy in the swim, crappy on the bike and really crappy on the run,' I told one reporter. The Olympics had left me feeling that way too.

It was like a grieving process and for a long time the feeling of utter failure didn't leave me. When you fall, it's the people closest to you who pick you up; family, close friends, and Marisa. At my lowest she was always there to remind me that I was still a good athlete, still capable of beating anyone, that one race didn't mean I suddenly no longer had ability.

Many people, acquaintances and strangers, showed kindness. I arrived home from Sydney to find a Speight's in my letterbox along with a note from my neighbour (he's a southern man) saying, 'Life goes on'. I still have some of the cards and notes I was sent, including a 'Happy Book' of drawings from the kids in my niece's class at Titirangi Primary School. Only later, when I began to emerge from that dark time, did I realise how important Sydney was for me. It could have destroyed me; instead, it fuelled the fire for the next stage of my career. It's no consolation at the time, but I came to appreciate that you learn most from your greatest disappointments. Sydney taught me that the key to success is failure.

Realising that I loved the sport and wanted to carry on was one thing; whether I could afford to was another. I wasn't exactly hot property any more. Being a professional triathlete was the only job I'd ever had, and on the biggest, most visible world stage I'd been an ordinary one. All my focus had been channelled into that Olympic race. Sydney was to be the pinnacle of my life and career, and you don't often think of what will happen next, of what the consequences will be if you stuff up. It's as if a black curtain is hiding the future beyond, then suddenly you burst, unprepared, through to the other side.

After the race, the calls from my sponsors began. The first was Colin May, from bike company Avanti, pledging 100 per cent support. They were all supportive, with the exception of Subaru, who no longer wanted to be associated with me as I hadn't won a medal. That's the only time that a sponsor has dumped me. I know it's business but I was disappointed that they didn't have faith. It was the loyalty of the others that meant I could still keep racing. That's what made the difference when I wondered whether I should give up chasing my dream and get a 'normal' job.

Roger Mortimer

I never doubted that Hamish had the ability to get back to the top. What I wasn't sure about was his desire. He calls the Games the ultimate gamble. You're shooting your whole life for one moment. If it comes off, you're the happiest man alive, a hero. If it doesn't, you fail and you're nothing. It's as simple as that. You can put a PR spin on it and you can rationalise it, but it *is* that clear cut. You either win or you don't.

Post-Sydney wasn't a great time to be marketing Hamish Carter. I wasn't enthusiastic about diving back into the sponsorship market for him until he started to prove himself again, and my advice was that he had to do some hard yards. I'm not sure that many manager-client relationships survive that sort of advice. Sometimes, as a manager, you have to tell it like it is, tell them they're not ready to get the big dollars because they're not ready as an athlete. Hamish certainly wasn't ready in 2001.

There was one meeting where I was talking about Sarah and Hamish to a representative of the sports drink Mizone. An executive from Mizone's advertising agency leant over the table and said to the client, 'Don't touch Hamish Carter, he's damaged goods.' I thought, 'You bastard. You'll live to regret that.' The ironic thing is that Mizone ended up having a relationship with Bevan Docherty, who came second in Athens. That's good, but they could have had a relationship with a guy who's become one of the great fight-back stories.

I have such respect for the people at Avanti, Vodafone and Nike who decided to stand by Hamish when he was down. At the time, the last public image of Hamish was of failure and despair, but I think that ad agency executive for Mizone made an extremely poor business decision. And I'd say that even if Hamish hadn't gone on to do what he did at Athens, because it was being a fair-weather friend. The greatest relationships Hamish and Sarah have now are with companies that backed them before they won at the Olympics — companies that liked who they were, liked their personalities as much as the image that they were great people doing great things. No athlete in the world can promise their sponsors that they're going to win an Olympic gold medal.

Roger went off and got a real job for a while and Susan Devoy, the former world squash star, helped me out with management tasks. During the summer following the Games, I mulled over what had gone wrong. First there was the selection fiasco, and then I hadn't handled the pressure of my first Olympics. Boardsailor Aaron McIntosh, who won a bronze in Sydney, made this point in response to Ineson's criticism: 'You can't prepare for the Olympic Games without an Olympic Games under your belt.'

In hindsight, I don't think my training was quite right. I didn't feel the lift you often get when you come down from altitude training. The idea is that you go somewhere about 2000 metres above sea level where there is less oxygen in the air. Your body compensates by producing more red blood cells, your oxygen-carriers. The first few weeks at altitude are tough but the pay-off comes when you return after a couple of months to the oxygen-rich air at sea level, where your enhanced ability to transport oxygen to your muscles provides an extra boost. When it's done right, it adds another weapon to your armoury, but it's another variable to factor in when you're trying to time your peak. You might feel good as soon as you come down to sea level, or it may kick in a week or two later. It's unpredictable and that time I don't think it worked.

In reality, I'd set myself up for a fall through my own expectations and by being too cocky for my own good. Years later, I discussed the dangers of expectation with my Aussie friend and great rival Greg Bennett and we agreed that it can be crippling. Greg's right when he says that you can only expect two things come race day: you're going to hurt and you'll do everything you can to draw out the best performance from yourself. I'd always spoken my mind to the media, but I got carried away with what I said. I know Roger thought I'd become too full of myself. It's something I talked to Rick Wells about later. His advice was to go easy with the talk and to let my deeds speak for me.

Rick Wells

Just about every successful athlete has had to eat humble pie at some time. I'm not a fan of being mealy-mouthed or of the Kiwi psyche where anyone who makes a bold statement gets jumped on. Sometimes you just can't win. I made the Commonwealth Games swimming team when I was 20 and living at home in the small rural town of Te Aroha. The local paper wanted to know if I was shooting for gold. There I was, up against all the Aussies, including the world record-holder; I was pleased just to have made the team, but the headline was 'Local boy shoots for gold'. I got eighth or ninth and broke the New Zealand record. I should have felt pretty proud, but instead I slunk around town as if I was a failure.

You live and learn. When I became one of the world's top triathletes, I took my lead from a Joe Walsh song: say what you think but never what you're planning.

Roger Mortimer

Talk is cheap. In my opinion there was an arrogance prior to Sydney. Hamish needed to get that out of his system and stop using phrases such as 'I'm bulletproof' and 'This is my destiny'. That's a load of rubbish. It's no one's right to win; no one's destiny.

It's one thing to have ambition and self-belief, but in those races you always struggle to manipulate the outcome. You need a degree of arrogance to believe that you can beat people, but to think that you have a divine right to win . . . I was embarrassed by talk like that. I didn't say anything at the time; we were young and I didn't have the confidence to pull him up. I do now, but it's no longer necessary; he learned that lesson himself. Talking about having a divine right is not the real Hamish — and there was none of that before Athens.

CLAWING BACK

They say that change can be like a renewal and I was about to go through a major period of change in my life. I was suddenly without Roger, who had been my navigator for so long, I knew I had to do something about my coaching, and I was about to become a family man.

Austin Harry Carter was born on 3 July, 2001. His timing was perfect. He was exactly what I needed, exactly when I needed it. I knew instinctively that it was the right time to start a family, even though the reality of doing so was a little scary given the uncertainty that Sydney had cast over my future earning ability as a professional athlete. And, added to that, of course, was that Marisa had to leave work to become a mum. I'm a very intuitive person and make a lot of big decisions on instinct, on whether something feels right. Buying the house with Marisa, getting married, starting a family; that all felt right. I'm intuitive when it comes to training, too. I don't automatically accept the status quo. If something has always been done a certain way, I'll look to see if there's a better one. It's when I lose my intuition that I'm all at sea and that tends to happen when I've been stressed.

Austin lifted what was a very flat year. Marisa believes our relationship might even have been damaged if Austin hadn't come along. She thought I needed a new focus in my life that was totally unrelated to triathlon.

Marisa

I got pregnant as soon as Hamish came back from Sydney. Suddenly, there was going to be something else for us to look forward to, and something that wasn't all about him — because you have to be very self-focused to compete at sport's elite level. I've been an athlete myself, so I understand that, but if you're with a partner who doesn't, it can be detrimental to the relationship.

Understanding it doesn't mean that it's not tough sometimes. I might have the kids to organise, the washing to get done, dinner to prepare — and there's Hamish sound asleep on the couch, recovering from a training session.

Austin's birth was quite something, although I guess all new dads say that. We'd planned it pretty much right down to the day, to fit in with my schedule. He was due in late June, but we decided that if he hadn't arrived by the beginning of July, the birth would be induced. As it turned out, we just made it. Four days after he arrived, I was on a plane to a World Cup race in Toronto with very mixed feelings. I knew it was my job, but after Austin's arrival I felt a bit shell-shocked and it was hard to concentrate on the business at hand. I felt that I shouldn't be leaving and I didn't want to go. Marisa, our families and friends were all urging me on, reassuring me that Marisa had plenty of support and that I wouldn't miss too much in the first six weeks of Austin's life. But I'd lost my usual passion for life as an athlete.

The bottom line was that I didn't know whether I could make it back to the top. If 2000 was the year of my greatest disappointment, 2001 was my year of greatest uncertainty. Life had flipped upside down. During that plane trip I thought about my new responsibility as a dad and tried to take stock. I had no idea how much longer I would remain in the sport.

Craig Watson was threatening my position as top Kiwi. He was beginning to consistently put in the fastest run, and sometimes beat me. I felt that I was slipping. On top of that, my team was becoming scattered. Roger and I had parted ways, and money was tight. I knew that it was time to move on from Jack, and I was struggling with an injured Achilles tendon, my worst injury for a long time. I was worried that it was a sign I was getting older and more injury-prone. A question mark hung over my ability to improve as an athlete. Perhaps the best was behind me.

After seven years in sports management, Roger had decided to take a break, and while I understood his decision, I missed him all the same. He still had the passion, but Sydney had affected us all; you take a hit when you don't do well at the Olympics, and the period after such a failure is tough. The money drops, and that's significant if you're getting only a percentage of the athlete's earnings. Sarah [Ulmer] had done okay, placing fourth in the pursuit in Sydney, but ours are not mainstream sports and there isn't much money in it unless you win the Olympics.

Then there was the issue of my coaching. I'd swum well in Sydney; swimming (for which Mark Bone was my coach) wasn't a problem. But I decided that time was up for Jack and me. I'd come a long way with him, but sometimes change is necessary. Telling him about this decision was one of the most difficult things I've had to do.

Jack Ralston

It took a long time for Hamish to get over Sydney, but I knew that once he headed overseas and back to the World Cup circuit his desire would return. In a way, he's an uncomplicated guy who likes an uncomplicated life, but he's also a very complicated guy, too. There's much more going on in his head than anyone knows. He'd been thinking about every aspect of his life as a professional athlete, including his coaching.

About a year after Sydney, he decided it was time we moved on. I admire him for being upfront about it. He came round home to tell me. It was sad, but that was his decision.

I rang Chris Pilone and asked him to work with me. Although, when he first became my coach, I wasn't completely sure whether it was going to work out, I knew the time was right to find out. I'd had a bit to do with him in the late 1990s, when I was running with Alan Bunce, and I liked his style, the way he communicated with his athletes, how he'd be down at the Auckland Domain on Wednesday nights, watching his guys do their sessions. They were little things, but little things that counted.

I've always played a strong hand in shaping my training and sometimes I tinker with the plan, occasionally even in the last few weeks before a big race. Over the years, I've learned what's right for me but I have a tendency to sometimes over-think things as a big race looms and I can lose my instinct. Chris could spot that. He'd ensure the fundamentals of my training were on track but would also allow me to be creative. When I came up with an idea, he'd usually say, 'Okay, we'll give it a try and see how it goes.' We'd then adopt what worked and discard the rest.

Switching to doing all three disciplines each day during the conditioning phase of my training was an example of how well we gelled as a partnership. I'd repeat that daily until I was exhausted and then do light recovery days until I was ready to load it up again. I would manage up to five days of heavy work, which bumped up my mileage, and then spend one to three days recuperating.

Coaches often have a clearer perspective than their athletes do, and Pilone and I seemed to bring out the best in each other. He knew when to rein me in and bring me back to where I needed to be. The final lead-in to a major race isn't the best time to pop in something you've never tried before, and once or twice when I wanted to change something, Pilone stood firm. By the same token, he was open to me challenging him with new ideas. With him as my coach, I found a happy medium.

Chris Pilone

After Sydney, I thought Hamish would race for perhaps another year and then flag it away, so I was surprised when he rang me in May 2001.

I was pretty green then, as a coach at top level. I'd had experience as a professional coach for the Millennium Institute of Sport and was coaching people who were borderline international level. But, even though I hadn't worked with a top international athlete, I had a feeling for what was required.

Not long after I started coaching him, Hamish went to the Edmonton World Championships carrying an injury and crapped out. I remember warning Marisa, even before Hamish got back, that there could be financial implications. He'd bombed at the Olympics and now at the world champs, and I wasn't sure whether he'd be able to keep going, because the injury meant that he couldn't do any serious running training.

He wanted to do the Goodwill Games, which were four weeks away, because there was big prize money up for grabs. I thought he'd be better to concentrate on getting over his injury and recommended he not go. But he did, and he got lucky. It was like winning Lotto. That was the turning point.

I wasn't sure I was doing the right thing by going to the Goodwill Games. Should I even be representing New Zealand when my injury meant that I couldn't race at 100 per cent? Some people thought it was a risk. If I bombed again, any aura of invincibility I might still have had for my younger Kiwi rivals would be completely destroyed.

Marisa thought I should race, not because I might make some money but because it was in my blood — because I'm an athlete and it's what I do. It was also the only thing that I *could* do. I wasn't qualified for any other job and it wasn't as if I had an inheritance or some other nest egg to fall back on. There's nothing more motivating than sheer desperation.

I went to that race in Brisbane with a different attitude. I wasn't going to out-run the field, but I was riding well. Pilone and I had compensated for my lack of quality running training by loading my cycling, including lots of races, but, because of my injury, I didn't have high expectations. Back when I was 15 and 16 and running cross-country races with my mates, I'd just go for it and see what eventuated. That's the attitude I took into the Goodwill Games. The lesson from Sydney, about the danger of expectation, was beginning to sink in.

I went off the front of the race and ripped it to bits — leading out of the water and taking off on the bike. Normally, I'd worry about whether I was doing the right thing using energy like that, with a pack cruising behind me like sharks at a fish restaurant. Chris McCormack joined me and I stopped thinking and just went for it. The first breakaway in a race gets caught 99 times out of 100, but this day we blitzed them, putting nearly three minutes on the pack. Macka won and I hobbled through the run for a clear second (the same one-two result as the 1997 World Championships), with Craig Watson once again smoking the run for third.

Macka was moving towards long-distance racing and had I been fully fit, I would have expected to out-run him. He seemed to think so, too, because during the bike he asked me to stay with him for the first couple of kilometres of the run before dropping him. He didn't know that I was carrying an injury. I'd kept quiet about it; there's no point letting your rivals know that you have a weakness. I didn't answer him — I don't speak when I'm racing, that way your rivals can't use it to read how you're feeling — but I knew that unless he was running like crap, he would beat me. It turned out that he wasn't in the best shape either, but we had such a big lead that the pack couldn't catch us.

It was a small but select field containing half a dozen world champions and Whitfield, the reigning Olympic champion. It was also an early taste of top international competition for a couple of rising young Kiwis, Bevan Docherty and Kris Gemmell, who finished 13th and 12th respectively. For me, it was one of those remarkable races where I wasn't the second-best triathlete in the field but I backed myself and it paid off.

I won US$30,000, which was a godsend for the young Carter family. But that wasn't the most important outcome. That race gave me back my confidence; I felt like I'd rediscovered my roots, my flair. The mistakes of Sydney suddenly seemed so clear: I'd become a very controlling athlete, wanting everything to be just right, and that had stifled the very essence of what made me a good triathlete. At the Goodwill Games, my injury forced me to focus on what I could do and to disregard the rest. I'd got my instinct back and it had seemed so simple.

That was an important note on which to finish such a tough year. As an athlete you can feel a hundred miles away from success, like you are teetering on the edge of a cliff, and then, out of nowhere, one race can bring you back on track. I had regained a sense of clarity and self-belief, and that gave me the confidence to experiment with my training and try different race tactics. Had I kept repeating my mistakes of Sydney, I wouldn't have made it to the next Olympic Games.

I felt that, at last, the dust of Sydney had settled. I'd got perspective, rediscovered the instinctive athlete that I naturally am, and felt my enthusiasm returning. Austin was a crucial part of that. Having a baby reset my life. Instead of looking back in disappointment, I started to look forward again, and there were some cool things ahead: 2002 was Commonwealth Games year and I'd never been to one before; the world championships were to be in Queenstown in 2003; and 2004 was Olympic year. I wanted to repay the faith my sponsors had showed in me by achieving something big for them, and also wanted to show Subaru that they had made a bad call in dropping me.

After Rog got back from Hawaii, where he'd completed the Ironman for about the fifth time, I went to see him and asked if he'd help me again. He was working an office job that he wasn't particularly enjoying and maybe he felt we had unfinished business together. He said yes and my team was complete; it was happy families again. I got to have a nice Christmas–New Year holiday with my new family thanks to my one decent race of 2001 at the Goodwill Games. I had my family, my manager back and a new coach. I returned to training ready to begin a new chapter. It was time to turn this ship around.

Chris Pilone

Hamish still harboured baggage about the Sydney Olympics selection process. I told him there was one way to deal with that: win the Oceania champs to gain automatic selection for the Commonwealth Games. By the time that race came around in March, he was relatively free of injury and we'd started to get a good idea about the right training for him.

Marisa

It was an important race, carrying Games selection and doubling as the New Zealand championships. He'd got a lucky break at the Goodwill Games, but people were still wondering if he was capable of making a comeback after Sydney.

Austin, who was eight months old, had a bug when we were in Queenstown and was very unwell. I tried to keep him away from Hamish as much as possible and spent time with Roger to give Hamish some space. Before the race Roger said to me, with real certainty in his voice, that one day Hamish would become one of New Zealand's best-ever athletes. Roger always had complete belief in him.

Despite the lift the Goodwill Games gave me, I wasn't the same athlete I was before Sydney, when my driving force had been built around the absolute conviction that I was destined to win that race. I had to get my head around the fact that the Olympic Games weren't mine by right, but something I had to go out and fight for.

I no longer had the same belief in myself and sometimes it just felt like a chore. When I started training in 2002, I was still very much a struggling athlete. Sydney was like a shackle. Each time my name was mentioned in the media, so was that race. Carter and failure in Sydney had become synonymous. Either I'd turn the corner and recapture my status as a top athlete or I'd fade away completely. That's why 24 March, 2002 was such an important day for me.

The importance of that race in Queenstown was foremost in my mind as I stood on the start line. I had followed the Olympics with a bad race at the world champs. If I failed here, I'd be history. In Sydney, I'd been full of angst about winning a gold medal. Now I just thought about doing a good swim, a good bike and a good run. I had learnt to focus only on what I could control. That sounds simple when you write it down, but it was like baring my soul. Somehow, I had to find the guts to stand there at the start of a big race in my own country and accept the prospect of being beaten.

I'd finally understood that you have to let a race go before you can get it back. It had taken me years to figure that out. Back in my school days, the biggest challenge that my rowing coaches faced was getting me to relax. I was so intense in my desire to do things better and harder that I actually slowed down myself and the boat, because when you're too tense, your natural rhythm is stifled. When you're relaxed, you are far more efficient. But that letting go involves such a leap of faith.

I'd learnt the most important lesson of my career: to separate my dream from my daily reality. Dreams are important and give you a sense of belief in yourself. But although a dream gives you direction, you can't wrap yourself in it or it will eat you alive. When a race flowed, it felt so easy; but if I filled my head with all the things that might go wrong, it would seem such a struggle. One approach crushes you; the other sets you free.

I was surprised by how easily I won the Oceania championship. Six of us rode away during the hilly bike leg — 2000 world champion Marceau, Shane Reed, the young brigade of Kieran Doe, Gemmell and Docherty, and myself. Early in the run I found myself alone in the lead and eventually crossed the line, clear by 40 seconds. I couldn't remember the last time I'd won by such a margin. It was an emphatic victory and I owe Rog for that. He knew what it meant. 'We needed that,' he said after I crossed the line. 'We needed that big time.' Compared with an Olympics, it wasn't a race to get excited about, but I had had everything to lose.

It's a race I will never forget and a lot of things made it special. It was held at Millbrook, near Queenstown, in awesome countryside and it was a stunningly beautiful day. The pictures and television footage looked spectacular and I remember the crowd being very loud. They like to see someone knocked off their perch, but they're also stoked when someone refuses to give up the fight and I felt the crowd sensed that in me.

I ran the last lap around the grounds of Millbrook knowing I had the race, my qualification, the Oceania champs and the national champs all sewn up. I could have cruised but Rog had cut across to the back of the course and was urging me on. I could hear it in the tone of his voice: I didn't just need to beat these guys, I needed to crush them. I had to make a statement. 'Carter demolishes quality opposition', the headlines read. It wasn't the biggest race in the world but right then it meant the world to me.

One of my overwhelming feelings was relief, because the hardest thing about the Olympics and Commonwealths isn't the games themselves, but qualifying. Under the standard required by Triathlon New Zealand, there are two qualifying races and in the first race you have to be the first or second Kiwi across the line. You're up against guys you might have beaten 50 times before, but on the day reputations count for nothing.

Often you're not trying to win the race but to cover one or two key people. Many strong challengers miss qualifying simply because the pressure has got to them. A poor swim or a puncture and it's all over. Because of the depth of talent, the New Zealand and Australian teams are the hardest to make. By the same token, people can came out of nowhere to qualify; Ben Bright for the Sydney Olympics and Nathan Richmond for Athens. I suspect there'll be a surprise for Beijing too. In Queenstown, I'd handled that pressure well and also coped with Austin being sick. Something like that can tip you over if you're feeling under pressure and worrying about catching something, but I accepted it as one of those things that I had no control over. In a way, having kids helped me let go of my need to control everything because, as anyone who has kids will know, you've got no choice but to go with the flow.

Three weeks after the race in Queenstown, I was third in Geelong, Australia, in the opening round of the World Cup. It was enough to push me to the top of the points table. Eighteen months after my disaster at the Olympic Games, I was once again ranked number one in the world.

The Commonwealth Games, in August, became the primary goal of my year. The world championships were in Cancun and I had no real ambition for them because the heat doesn't seem to suit me. But I also wanted to target the Lifetime Fitness Triathlon in Minneapolis. It was the first time the event had been held, with a unique format. Billed as the battle of the sexes, men and women compete alongside each other, with the women given a carefully calculated head start. There was good prize money up for grabs, including a pot of about

US$100,000 on the line for the outright winner. Mathematicians were hired to formulate the women's start, taking into account all sorts of things such the 10 km world running records and the winning times at the Sydney Olympic triathlon. The formula they created was called 'the equaliser'. It was a really cool idea and attracted most of the big names of our sport.

It was the first time since the rebel series in 1996 that the ITU had been challenged, and it reacted by threatening sanctions against athletes who competed in the race. But we didn't have contracts preventing us from racing, so it was a free market and we jumped at the chance to race for some good money. The ITU had treated the athletes like rubbish over the years, so loyalty wasn't an issue. There was an ITU World Cup race on the same weekend and the ITU made a snap decision to double the world series points just for that one race to try to lure athletes away from the Lifetime Fitness Triathlon — a classic example of the dubious decisions it sometimes made. In my book, it showed that the ITU lacked credibility, changing the structure of a World Cup series at the stroke of a pen. Besides, double points didn't exactly put bread on your table. There wasn't any money up for winning the overall series.

My decision to make the Commonwealth Games — a race with no prize money — the top priority of my year was a big call financially, especially as history shows it's almost impossible to do well at the Commonwealth Games and the world championships in the same year. After failing at the Olympics and the last worlds, my Government funding was near zero. Lifetime Fitness was my chance to earn some money for the year, but it was two weeks before the Commonwealth Games and Pilone was pretty dubious. He would have preferred us to stick to the usual plan and do key training sessions to bring me to a peak for the Games in Manchester. That's how my creativity worked alongside Chris's tendency to bring me back to basics. With Jack, I felt ready two to four weeks before a targeted event and as if I was trying to hold on to my form; with Pilone it would seem we hardly had enough time. A month out from the target race and every session had to count. It created an urgency that worked for me, because I'd hit my peak not a moment too soon.

I thought we could leave out some of those major training sessions and bank on the Lifetime race to bring me up for the Commonwealth Games. Pilone was far from convinced and, to be honest, I didn't have a lot of confidence in my decision either. But I'd gone to Sydney with the perfect build-up and bombed. Maybe if I did something crazy, it just might come off.

I had a good race, although I wasn't flying, finishing seventh overall and fifth male. The guys held back too much during the bike and the Australian triathlete Loretta Harrop won. I flew straight on to the Games village in Manchester. The challenge now was to recover from the Lifetime race and settle in to village life.

The triathlon was scheduled for the last day of competition, so I had two weeks in the Games village. Each day I'd do a light swim, ride and run, which meant going through six security checks as I came and went from the village. When you wanted to eat, it was a 15-minute walk to the food hall. Living anything like a normal life there is almost impossible, but I had two things going for me. Sydney had taught me that I had to chill and go with the flow. And I met Dave Currie for the first time.

Dave was Chef de Mission of the New Zealand team. After my experience with Les Mills in Sydney, I wasn't looking forward to meeting Dave, but, amazingly, instead of giving us a list of rules, he told us to go ahead and do whatever we needed to race well. If that meant disappearing into the countryside for a week, we were free to leave the village. It was exactly what I wanted to hear. At last, I felt I was in a team where the priority was getting the best from the athletes.

I trained during the day and watched events in the evening. It kept me busy and meant I didn't have a lot of time to spend worrying about my race. That was another difference between Pilone and Jack. With Jack I'd do very little in the week before race day, but Chris had me doing long sessions with minimal intensity. When you're very fit that's easy, but it does occupy your days. It was a good call, because your body can respond to a dramatic drop in workload by almost shutting down and leaving you feeling tired or off colour. Four days out from the race I did a 90-km ride but cruised it, chatting to people all the way. It was actually relaxing, and I arrived at the start of my race fizzing to get stuck in.

I led the first part of the swim and then cruised on Simon Lessing's heels. It was one of the noisiest swims I've done. Each time I turned my head to take a breath I got a snapshot of the wharf lined with people with their mouths wide open shouting and it struck me how funny they looked. Taking in that sort of thing was a good sign; it meant I was relaxed.

Peter Robertson and Gemmell took off at the beginning of the run and were chased by Miles Stewart and Lessing. I couldn't go with them, which was worrying, because if they'd sustained that pace the race would have been gone. After a kilometre, I was lying fifth or sixth. A top-10 finish is an average result at the Commonwealth Games and I wasn't happy that Gemmell, a Kiwi, was off up the road. But I didn't panic. I was running well and feeling good; it was a matter of concentrating on my rhythm, and seeing what transpired.

Simon Whitfield, who had won in Sydney, came past me but I was picking my way through the field too. Robbo and Gemmell blew up, and Lessing also faded. Suddenly, there were three: Whitfield, chased by Stewart and me. I pushed as hard as I could for the last 3 km hoping to drop Stewart and stop Lessing catching us, because both have potent finishing kicks. I finished so strongly that we almost caught Simon. I was third, just seven seconds behind the Sydney Olympic champion. I was delighted with my race, particularly on a dead-flat course that did me no favours.

Chris Pilone

Even after he got third in the Commonwealth Games there was never any vision on my part that he might win an Olympic medal. As a coach I was trying to proceed in small steps. We learnt an important lesson that year. Hamish had done the Oceania champs to get selected for the Commonwealth Games, peaked again for that, then tried to peak a third time for the worlds in Cancun at the end of the year. It was too much and he finished well back at Cancun.

I was hugely encouraged by my result at the Commonwealth Games.

Unlike my previous selection drama, I'd qualified without a hitch. We'd got the training right, I'd peaked for the race and I'd handled that bloody Games village environment. With Chris's coaching, I felt we were beginning to figure the sport out. The medal was nice, but the real reward was what it meant for me psychologically.

My bronze was the only medal the triathletes won at Manchester and I was proud to have contributed to New Zealand's tally. I've always been motivated by representing my country and get almost the biggest kick from the enjoyment people (even strangers) get from my successes. After the devastation of Sydney, I discussed that with John Hart, the former All Black coach, who I met at a corporate event. We were talking about motivation and I told him that one of the most influential factors for me was the pleasure it gave people when I won. I said that was one reason why I could face another Olympics. John warned me that I couldn't live like that, because taking on the responsibility for the spirit of an entire nation is enough to crush anyone. Who would understand that better than an All Black coach and, in hindsight, I think that was a factor in what happened to me in Sydney. I realised that if I made it to the Olympics again, it had to be for myself — to produce a performance I could be proud of for its own sake.

First, I had to win selection. In 2003 a brat pack was coming through that was bigger and stronger than the one I'd been part of at the beginning of my career, when all I had wanted was to knock off Rick Wells. Now *I* was the target. Lining me up in their sights were the ultra-talented young ones, such as Terenzo Bozzone, the world junior champion for whom great things were being predicted, and Nathan Richmond, who Pilone was coaching. Then there was Gemmell (fifth and first Kiwi at the 2002 worlds) and Docherty, who had served their apprenticeships and were ready to strike. Some media were suggesting Bozzone would be first choice for Athens; one article predicted Gemmell would become New Zealand's top triathlete during 2003 and that I would retire.

It was mentally challenging to have guys who I used to drop like a bad habit snapping at my heels. For years, I'd never seen Bevan in a race, then suddenly he's running right alongside me, and it wasn't because my standard had dropped. As Olympic year drew closer, there was a view in some quarters that I'd had my chance in Sydney and it was time for me to move aside.

Bevan Docherty

> My good friend Kris Gemmell and I would joke about Hamish being the old man, the old bugger. It might come across as a lack of respect but it's actually the reverse, because your whole goal is to knock the number one off.
>
> One of the reasons I got so good was because as a junior all I wanted was to beat Hamish. Everything was focused towards that, and when I achieved it, his personality was to strike back. It was a dogfight. You could say that we were productively competitive because our rivalry compelled us to get the best out of ourselves and made us both better athletes.

The race chosen as the Olympic selection trial was the world championships in Queenstown, only the second time it had been held in New Zealand. The first two Kiwis to finish gained automatic selection, as long as they finished in the top 20. Selectors choose a big race so they can gauge you against the best, but it ruins the chance of a Kiwi winning because that becomes secondary to bagging a qualifying spot. If Gemmell or I tried to break away on the bike, the other Kiwis would chase the move down. And that's pretty much how the race went. Olivier Marceau and Robbo got away on the bike while all the Kiwis marked each other. None of us was prepared to put everything into chasing them, in fear of paying for that effort during the run and fading out of contention for the Olympics. It's a bit sad, because everyone would love to see a Kiwi win the world championships in our own country, but getting to the Olympics is more important.

Bevan finished fourth and I was fifth — booking our tickets to Athens, the city where the history of the Olympics began. Even though Bevan had beaten me, my overwhelming emotion, as I sat on the grass with Austin after the race, was relief. I didn't have to train as if my life depended on it for another trial in two months, to fight for the third place in the team. Instead, I'd get to enjoy a family break over Christmas.

I totally understood when Craig Watson decided to retire rather than carry on for the last selection race in Tasmania. Craig was the unlucky one. He ran faster than both Bevan and me in Queenstown and finished sixth, one place away from automatic selection. In theory, he would have been a certainty for the last place in the team, but he'd made the decision to retire if he didn't qualify at the world champs and he stuck to it. After a long career, he'd had enough. That you can get sixth at the world championships and yet not get selected shows how strong New Zealand was in triathlon at the time. Craig is as nice a guy as you could meet, and he was missed. There were more talented guys around but few could match his work ethic. There were a couple of years where he was possibly fitter than all of us, and he really deserved the world championship medal he won in 2001.

A purist who loved to train and race, he wasn't big on marketing himself and deserved to earn a lot more from the sport than he did. Some years earlier, when his racing flats (shoes) were worn out, I gave him a spare pair of Nikes. In the next race the bugger passed me and I had to endure the frustration of watching him draw away wearing my damned shoes! But Craig was always willing to help. Even though he wasn't in the team for Athens, he found and booked our Olympic training camp in Pau. He's married to a French woman and lives locally, so knew the area well.

I was ready to hit Pauanui and the beach for a well-earned break. It had been a long, hard year. Instead of the season running as usual, from March to September, the world championships were in December. That meant that we had to change our usual plan for the season to make sure I wasn't burnt out by then. I had a couple of weeks off in the middle of the season, but it was also a period when Chris and I were reinventing my training. As I got older, I didn't respond so well to too much high-intensity training.

I felt we were getting the training right and it had been a very good year as far as results went. I'd won a few races, including a World Cup race (Corner Brook, Canada) and I'd qualified for the Olympics without any drama. It was a relief for the whole family.

Professional athletes lead a roller-coaster life and it affects everyone close to you. My moods can set the tone for the whole household and I'd put the family through the wringer trying to qualify for Sydney. Marisa was probably even more relieved than I was when I qualified in Queenstown; she was six months pregnant. That was our big news of the year: Austin was going to have a baby sister. That's another thing about being a professional athlete — it even dictates planning a family. We'd timed having Phoebe with Athens in mind.

Marisa

It was another full-on year: Hame was overseas for three months, renovations dragged on for nine months and were finished the week of the world champs. But somehow the timing always seemed to work out. He didn't win in Sydney, then Austin came along the next year at the right time for Hamish to do the Goodwill Games. With Phoebe, we had a one-month window to conceive if we were to have our next baby before Athens, because I didn't want to have a newborn and a toddler when Hamish would be going away for three months to prepare for the Games. My midwife was away in February, so the baby had to arrive in March. That was the window, and it happened. Phoebe was born on 12 March. It's the way Hamish's life seems to happen. Things do fall into place. Sometimes you wonder if there's some grand plan.

It was an enormously satisfying year considering that I'd struggled to maintain motivation and sometimes felt retirement might be just around the corner. My dream was still there, but having a family helped put it into perspective. They gave me the balance I needed and I felt I was better equipped to face the Olympics this time round. It might be that it would end in disappointment, but I no longer saw it purely as an all-or-nothing situation. I desperately wanted to win, but I looked at it as a second chance to do justice to the Olympic Games. That was my mission, to be able to say I'd done all I could to chase my dream.

THE NEARLY MAN

When I won the bronze medal at the 1993 world championships after just two years in the sport, I had expected it wouldn't be long before I could write 'World Champion' on my CV. I'd come far in short order, I was improving steadily and I had the confidence of youth. But 11 years later here I was, still waiting. I'd won plenty of World Cup races, won the World Cup series, had a long run as the world's top-ranked triathlete, but a world title still eluded me. My world champs record read: second, third, fourth, fourth, fifth, fifth, sixth, ninth. Though consistent, it had gained me a reputation no athlete wants. I'd become 'the nearly man'. The bridesmaid. An Olympic title stands above all sports accolades and 2004 was Olympic year, my chance — perhaps my last chance — to write a better epitaph.

To the athletes, a world championship in Olympic year is a secondary event. Pilone and I had to build a season to peak for Athens — Athens and only Athens. Come Thursday 26 August, I had to be in better shape than I had ever been at any time in my life. The key to timing your peak is a couple of crucial, hard training sessions. We decided to hold them off until August, within a month of the race. When you do these sessions, you suddenly peak up and are ready to rock. It's rare for an athlete to reach a high peak twice in a season, particularly an older athlete, as I was at 33. The worlds were in Madeira, Portugal, in early May. You certainly can't hold a peak from May until August. If I was racing at 100 per cent in May, I was going to be toast by the time the Olympics come around.

I knew I had only one shot at reaching my absolute peak fitness. I'd learnt that lesson in 2002 when I peaked for the Commonwealth Games and then tried to come up again for the world champs in Cancun a few months later and completely bombed. In fact, all three medallists from those games — Simon Whitfield, Miles Stewart and myself — were toast at the worlds. Stewart was first home in 48th place. Next Commonwealth Games, same thing. The medallists then were Brad Kahlefeldt, Bevan Docherty and Peter Robertson. At the worlds, the first two didn't finish while Robbo managed sixth. It's just how the sport works. Sometimes an athlete can fluke it, but nine times out of 10, if you're dynamite at the start of the season, you're a dud by the end.

We decided to go to Madeira not because we thought I had a chance to win but because I could check out the Athens course on my way home. Another factor was that the worlds carry double World Cup ranking points, which are used to prioritise the selection of positions on the start pontoon for the Olympics. Pilone told me to aim for a top-10 or top-15 finish, collect some points, and then we'd get on with the part of the year that really counted.

In Madeira, there was a muck-up at the start. They tried to stop Kris Gemmell, another of the Kiwis, and me starting because we were wearing only Speedos. Apparently you weren't allowed to race bare-chested, although it wasn't mentioned at the race briefing. The gun went and we dived in anyway. I had a good swim but an official in the transition area waved a yellow card at me, signalling a 15-second stand-down penalty. Kris was stopped, too. We were standing there watching our rivals streaming past and Kris began arguing, so the official said, 'Your 15 seconds starts again!' I was almost laughing at the absurdity of it. But that incident kicked off a theme for 2004. I had a lot of things like that go against me.

It's hard to be in a big race knowing that you've only done endurance training and don't have the necessary sharpness, but Kris and I caught the lead pack on the bike. Halfway through the run I was fifth, which meant, all things considered, that I was having an absolute blinder. I should have been fired up about that, but all I could think of was that Bevan was up front. I didn't want him to win this race. As it came toward the finish, I could see the leaders 20 or 30 seconds ahead as they approached the finish chute. It was going to be a sprint. It was as though I'd forgotten about my own race. I was obsessed about the possibility of Bevan winning; that after so many years I was no longer 'the man'.

I heard the crowd roar so knew it was a close finish, but I didn't think he'd out-sprint the Spaniard, Ivan Rana. I was so busy obsessing about Bevan that I dropped a place in the last kilometre and finished sixth. Any other day, that would have been an incredible result considering my preparation. But when I crossed the line, I saw Bevan leaping around like a loon and thought, 'He's won'. He was the centre of the world and I was just devastated. I walked off, while the rest of the New Zealand team did the haka, and rang Roger in New Zealand to tell him the news. He didn't flinch and calmly told me that it was the best thing that could have happened.

'C'mon, what are you talking about?' I said.

'Trust me, it's the best thing that could have happened.'

Then I phoned Pilone. 'That's perfect,' he said. 'What are you talking about?' I ranted back at him. 'Bevan just kicked my arse and won the world champs. I've been doing this sport for 13 years and I've never won the world champs. He's never even won the national champs. He won his first World Cup race two weeks ago. I've won 10. It's not fair.'

I stomped off to the transition area, where my bike and gear were, feeling sorry for myself. I was filled with anger at the injustice of it all. I'd done so much over so many years without nailing the big one and I'd just got beaten by this young kid who'd come out of nowhere to do everything I'd ever wanted to do. I sat down on the plastic bin they give you to store your clothes in and the damn thing collapsed under my weight. I went sprawling on my arse just as Debbie Tanner and a couple of other young Kiwi girls walked past.

They stopped laughing when they saw the look on my face. I'd been 'the man' for so long, carrying the beacon for New Zealand in triathlon. Suddenly everyone was buzzing about Bevan and here was I, sprawled on the ground like an idiot.

It sounds ungracious but I didn't think he deserved it. It should have been me up there. He hadn't served an apprenticeship. But in sport there's no such thing; there are no rules about having to pay your dues. Chris and Roger were like, 'Brilliant, it's so crucial that happened.' I just couldn't see it.

Chris Pilone

I got a phone call from Hamish in Madeira. Even before he told me how he went, he said, 'Bloody Docherty won the world champs. I've never won the world champs.' I think he added, 'And I never will.' After he got back to Auckland we met up and put it in perspective. He'd finished sixth off build-up training. How far was he behind Bevan? Thirty-seven seconds. That was perfect. I firmly believed he had to aim only for Athens: one build-up, one goal. Later, Mark Elliott told me that at certain stages before Athens, Bevan was almost at the end of his tether, just hanging on to his form, whereas Hamish was really coming on.

I drowned my sorrows a bit that night. As a team-building exercise we'd decided to rent scooters and do a bit of sightseeing, but half the team turned up worse for wear. We had to get coffees and sober up before we went tearing off. It was mayhem. No licences, no worries — such is the Kiwi way. I enjoyed it despite myself, but I wasn't happy. The next day we flew to Athens to look at the Olympic course. Bevan was like a different guy. His confidence had grown so much, it was like he'd plugged a cable into me, drained all the power out and pumped it into himself. I was like this fading has-been and he was the rock star.

I liked what I saw in Athens. The bike course had a steep climb that we'd race over five times. As I rode it, I started to get excited. It was a tough course, on a beautiful piece of coastline out of Athens, where biking ability would count. You would need to be a true triathlete to do well here.

It was while I was checking the venue that I realised I had to start thinking about what I could do and forget the rest. That was a key lesson from Sydney, where I'd worried about everything to the point of my own destruction. But it was a lesson I'd yet to learn because there I'd been in Madeira, in the final kilometre of the world champs, worrying about what someone else was doing. I boarded the plane for home in a better frame of mind. It was nice to feel excited about the course because there'd been the possibility that seeing it would bring the disappointment of Sydney flooding back and fill me with terror about going to another Olympics. I started to realise that it was up to me to turn these negatives into positives. No one could do it for me.

Chris and Roger's views were sinking in too. If Bevan was on fire now, surely he was going to fizzle out later. That was reinforced when I got home because Marisa could see the silver lining too. I had a short break and then the build-up to Athens began in earnest.

Eight weeks before the Olympics, I packed my bags, kissed Marisa, our three-year-old Austin and baby Phoebe, and flew to Edmonton for a World Cup race, the first step on the home straight to Athens. But there was a storm and the race was cancelled. That was frustrating, because each race is a vital step in your preparation, and that's intensified in Olympic year. It annoyed me that I'd been away for 10 days for nothing. I could have spent that time at home with Phoebe, who was just three months old.

Next up was Lifetime Fitness, the big-money race in Minneapolis. In the back of my mind was a little spark of hope that if I raced well there, I could afford to fly Marisa and the kids to Pau in the south of France, my training base for the final weeks leading up to the Games. Having them there for a few weeks would have made me much happier because I've always missed home, especially since having kids. First prize was $150,000, but a top-five placing would have been enough.

I was racing along on the bike, feeling good, when a marshal called me for drafting. Lifetime is a non-drafting race. The rules state that you have to stagger on the bike, which means not riding in a direct line behind the rider in front, no matter how far behind you are. We were on a windy and narrow part of the course, chasing two guys up the road. I'd been trying to bridge up to them, riding the tangents of the corners, and may have been in line for a second or two, although too far back to have made any difference. I had to stand on the side of the road for a minute watching the race and my hopes of flying the family to France disappear up the road. It ripped me. The world champs, Edmonton and now this. Bevan came fourth. I still had a good race, finishing eighth with the third-fastest run. But I felt as though nothing would go right. It was like a knife in the guts.

The draft busters are guys you just want to kill. They wear black-and-white striped vests like an umpire in American football and are so self-righteous. I guess they're just doing their job. The one who stopped me was a guy named Charlie. I saw him at the Lifetime Fitness race the following year and told him, 'You gave me a penalty for drafting and it almost ruined my life because my wife couldn't come over for the Olympics. But you know what? You were one of the key reasons why I won the gold medal, because I got so pissed off, I went and trained so hard.' Tears actually welled up in his eyes. He said he'd never ever been told something good had come out of a drafting penalty.

I was still angry when I got to Pau. My response was to get into some massive training. Pilone was there to make sure I didn't destroy myself, making sure I had adequate recovery time.

Chris Pilone

He wasn't in a totally level frame of mind when he arrived in Pau. I found out later about how his hopes of bringing Marisa over had been dashed. Early on in the camp, he came storming in, as he periodically did during our relationship, and said, 'Pilone, you've got to drop some of the bike work and stack the training towards the run.'

I disagreed, but I was conscious that Hamish had been racing the World Cup circuit for 12 years and I'd never done a triathlon in my life and had coached very few triathletes. I'd also not seen the course. 'God, Hamish,' I said, 'I think you might be wrong here. It's a very tough bike course and it's going to be very hot as well.' I told him I thought that a group would ride away and it would be a fight for survival, that a run of 32 minutes flat off the bike would do it. The key was strength rather than speed.

He took some convincing. We worked it through with pencil and paper. The last month of Carter's Olympic training programme was scribbled on a piece of A4 paper — hardly the sort of thing you would present at a sports coaching conference. I wrote down what we needed to emphasise and he wrote down the sessions required to achieve them. He needed to be able to run fast, with a relaxed rhythm, he needed strength and endurance on the bike, plus the explosiveness to cover attacks on the hill, and because he's a bit of a diesel engine, we needed to maintain aerobic strength for both the bike and run. That meant controlled hill efforts of 10 or 15 minutes each on the bike, 90-second power-climbing efforts for explosiveness, and some long runs and rides. There was only one lead-up race to go, four weeks out, and we decided he needed to do a big race-specific session off the bike two weeks out from race day. This session would be done at a higher intensity than in a race.

Bevan was in camp. There were camera crews coming and going. Every day he was doing an interview. Little by little I started to go inside myself, to sit back and observe all this, watching him play the media game. He loves it and it works for him, it kinda fuels his fire. I'd done exactly the same before the Sydney Olympics and it was part of my undoing. This time, no one wanted to talk to me. I didn't have to chat about how my training was going, didn't have to answer any questions about myself. The occasional time a call came in for me, I put them on to Bevan. He loved it because he could do it, and I loved it because I didn't have to do it. Day by day, bit by bit, my confidence grew.

Bevan's win at the worlds definitely spurred me on and so did the media coverage. I'd been *Sports Illustrated* magazine's pick to win in 2000. This time the magazine was tipping Bevan to win gold. I'd disappeared off the radar. Each time I saw Bevan in the media, my desire to beat him rose. He was taking over my mantle and I wanted to be top dog again. It had become personal. In Queenstown, after the previous year's world champs, where he beat me in a big race for the first time (he was fourth, I was fifth), he'd said that I had 'been a great athlete but it's time for [Carter] to move over'. Simon Whitfield told me that on the start line in Madeira. I used these things as a powerful motivator.

Photosport

The World Cup in Sydney, 1998. I'm going off the front with Chris Hill in hot pursuit.

Photosport

Another Sydney World Cup: this one in 1997 — the easiest win I ever had.

Photosport

World Cup in Auckland, 1998. It's magic winning on your home track.

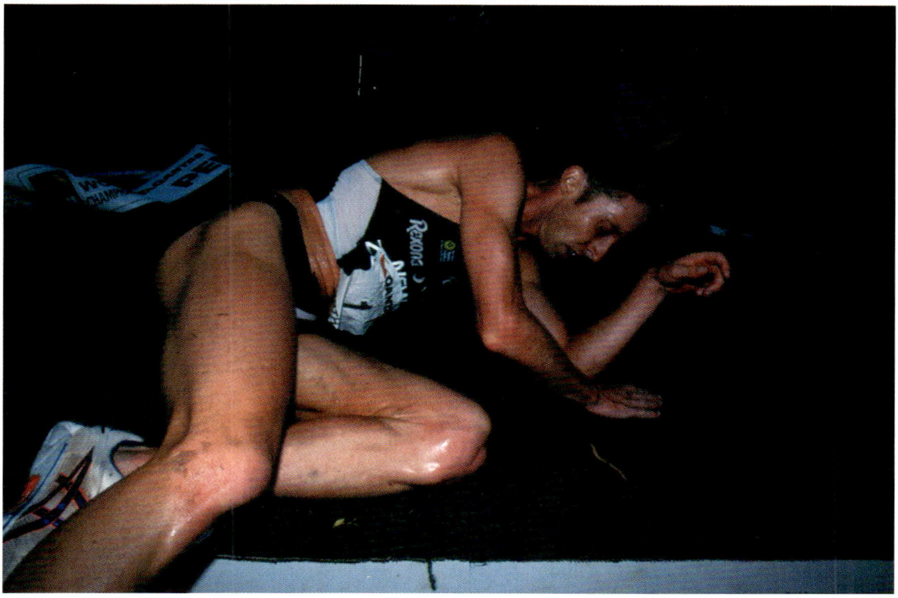

Photosport

2000 World Champs: I passed out on the finish line, but I had qualified for the Sydney Olympics.

Photosport

Swim exit at Lake Hayes, Queenstown, during the 2002 Oceania and New Zealand Championships.

Photosport

Same race: I break away on the bike, with Olivier Marceau close behind.

Photosport

Running away in the last leg in Queenstown, 2002.

Photosport

Photosport

SYDNEY OLYMPICS
ABOVE: Ugly photo on an ugly day.
ABOVE, RIGHT: 'Honey, can I go shopping now?'

RIGHT: Happier times: winning the bronze at the Commonwealth Games in Manchester, 2002.

Photosport

Photosport

Athens, 2004: Leading with Bevan Docherty close behind, and Sven Riederer in 3rd place.

Photosport

On the winner's podium.

Photosport

Me and Chris Pilone (white cap) backstage in Athens with the drug-testing chaperone.

Photosport

Carrying the New Zealand flag was my personal highlight from the 2006 Melbourne Commonwealth Games.

Photosport

Racing for New Zealand at my final World Championships in Lausanne, 2006.

Photosport

The end is nigh . . . I've just finished second in Lausanne. For all intents and purposes this was my final outing on the world stage.

Even though we were both staying in the team house, Bevan and I hardly ever trained together. I didn't think about it at the time, but we'd head out on a training ride and he'd turn left and I'd turn right. I trained with the young guys, Nathan Richmond, the third member of the three-man Olympic triathlon team, and Liam Scopes who was my running buddy. Bevan had his guys, such as Kris Gemmell. Pilone reckons he had to separate Bevan and me otherwise we would have worked each other over in training in an attempt to gain some sort of psychological advantage.

Chris Pilone

The Carter–Docherty rivalry would be one of the biggest in New Zealand sport. Bevan's coach was Mark Elliott, Triathlon New Zealand's high performance manager, but it never affected our relationship. Mark and I functioned well and started to conspire so that Hamish and Bevan didn't train together. Otherwise we might have ended up with two corpses instead of two superbly fit athletes.

I reckon Carter blew Nathan Richmond's campaign, although that was my fault too. They trained together for the first couple of weeks in Pau. I could tell Hamish was going well but I didn't realise then quite how well. He started hammering Nathan and I didn't split them apart early enough. Even when I did, they'd go behind my back. One time Carter was to do a strength-endurance bike session — three efforts of 15-minutes each on the Col de Marie-Blanque, a category 1 climb that's used in the Tour de France. A group of us were riding up it but only Carter was to do the hard session, not Richmond, because he'd just returned from the Games' opening ceremony and was tired from the travel. I made that clear to both of them separately. On the ride, Richmond had stopped lower down the mountain and then Carter turned back, I assumed to have a leak. I rode on for another 10 minutes and then Carter and Richmond came steaming past. Carter had gone back to get him. It was a total balls-up.

I had my work cut out to make sure Hamish didn't overdo it on recovery days. The problem was that he'd get bored. One particular Monday was supposed to be an easy day, a swim in the morning and then a two-hour ride on the flat, on a ring road around Pau. It was pleasant riding but Hamish hates being on the flat. I was riding in front with Scopes, who is very proper and never rocks the boat. Hamish was riding 200 m behind and wasn't happy. After about 45 minutes he came up from his position behind and said, 'Look, we'll just turn up in to here. I know where I'm going.' We made the right-hander and the road immediately climbed. The further we went, the narrower and steeper it got, and before long the seal ended. It was stinking hot and I was gradually dropping behind, increasingly annoyed because it was supposed to be an easy day. At one point we rode through what appeared to be a farmer's bloody chook yard. Scopes dropped back to me and I said, 'Look Liam, Carter's got absolutely no idea where he is. In a minute the people on the side of the road will be speaking Spanish because I think that's where we are.'

By this stage I was ropable, but Carter was out of earshot further up the road. Eventually we came out onto a road I recognised and we took the most direct route home. But instead of the two-hour cruise I'd planned, we'd done nearly four hours of mountainous riding in the baking sun.

'It was a bit of a miscalculation,' said Carter, 'but it turned out okay.'

'What about the poor bastards with ya?' I replied. When we got home, I got a big bottle of Coke, put a chair in the shower and let the water run over me.

'I know where I'm going.' It became the standard joke. It's funny now, but I wasn't laughing then.

My final race before Athens was the City of London Triathlon. Pilone was playing down expectations but it was only a month until the Olympics and I thought I should be showing some form. I had a diabolical swim. I was getting quite skinny and that can affect your swimming. I didn't make it up to the lead group and began the run a minute down. Then I heard a familiar voice above the noise of the crowd. I recognised it as Brett Sutton, the hard-man Aussie coach from those Alpe d'Huez training camps all those years ago. The run was on a small circuit in the Docklands area of London and each lap I'd hear Sutton screaming at me, 'Use it, use this race.'

I knew exactly what he meant. Run as though it's the Olympics.

Chase those guys down. Make this race count. I ran through the field up to fourth. Finally I'd learnt to focus on my race, to make the most of any opportunity that came my way.

Bevan won, which would further fuel his confidence, but I felt a small swell inside of me. I hadn't been racing that well and I'd had some bad luck, but I could sense it was coming together. I'd done the fastest run, half a minute quicker than Bevan's. Being a minute down had become a worrying pattern. I was a minute down in London, a minute down after my draft penalty at Lifetime Fitness. It was demoralising, because you know that no matter how hard you push during the run, you're unlikely to make the final placings.

I returned to Pau from London feeling that I'd started to turn the corner. I'd always had a problem with being ready too early for big races. This time I might just be ready in time. From now, every day and every session counted. Whether it was a big, key session or an easy recovery day, it was vital they were all done right.

The opening ceremony was coming up. The triathlon was at the end of the games, almost two weeks later. I made what I now think was a crucial decision not to go to the opening. It would have involved an entire day travelling from Pau to Athens, two days there and then another day travelling back. Nathan and Bevan went. Instead, I did the biggest four days' training of my life. I had the camp to myself — just me, my coach and a handful of training hacks.

It was as though a truck came in each day and dumped coal on this fire inside me because I felt myself get stronger and stronger. On the fourth day I was to do my last key session, the most important of the season, maybe of my career, to kick me up to another level. The session had been planned for weeks. It was designed to be more challenging than any race and I had to nail it.

I started with a hard swim. Then I did a two-hour bike ride that included a hill I'd chosen because it was infinitely tougher than the one in Athens, so steep your front wheel almost lifts off the road. Pilone was out with a broom because if you rode over any gravel, your wheel would skid. We teased Pilone about that, told him we'd get him an apron to go with the broom so that he'd look the part of resident lackey. I did that climb 10 times, just belted myself. I finished the ride at the track in the middle of the day, and went straight into a running session of eight 1 km repetitions with 45 seconds' rest between. Scopes and Clark Ellice were there to pace me. They'd warmed up and were ready when I hopped off the bike and took turns pacing me, running 1 km and resting the next. There was no holding back.

I told Pilone not to tell me my times. My plan was to knock some off then push the last few as hard as I could. Halfway through, I asked him what times I was running and he brushed me off. I felt like I was moving well, smooth and relatively controlled, sitting behind my pacemaker. With three to go, Pilone said, 'This is going pretty well.' It was a total understatement because it turned out I was running 2:50–2:52, faster than I thought I'd ever be able to run.

Pilone had held off telling me my times until a point in the session where I was just about to crack. When I heard how fast I was running, it made me determined to bring those last three reps home. A few of the guys and girls from the Kiwi camp were watching and a bit of a buzz had developed. Kris Gemmell, who was Bevan's training hack, got so caught up in it that he stepped onto the track to pace me on the final one. I made it through the last three, running times that were still in the low 2:50s. I was just rooted, but enormously satisfied because I knew no one in the world had done a session like that, on that day. I thought, 'I don't care what happens at the Olympics now because with that under my belt, if someone beats me they're too good.'

Pilone just said, 'That went pretty well.'

'Pretty well?' I said. 'I thought it went bloody well actually.'

'Oh yeah,' he said. 'Pretty good, pretty good.' And he walked off leaving me thinking, 'You bastard, I buried myself on that session'.

Chris Pilone

I strongly believe there's got to be a bit of distance between coach and athlete. It's just as well Hamish is retiring because we've become too friendly since the Olympics. I don't think I said anything to Hamish, but after that session I was bloody certain he was going to win. He was absolutely flying. I said as much to Liam. It was like God sending you a telegram with advance warning of the next winner of the Melbourne Cup. That's when Liam decided he was going to go to

> Athens. He couldn't get a flight, so he took a boat, slept on the deck and turned up for the race.
>
> It was a bit of an eye-opener for me. I coach marathon runner Dale Warrander too, so I had three athletes who'd made it to the Olympics and I'd got a free trip to Athens as assistant to Mark Elliott to see them race. It was already a win for me. Then suddenly, exactly two weeks out, I realised Hamish was probably unbeatable.

After a brutal session like that you have to make sure you recover well. Normally, the next day I'd just sit around the apartment with my feet up but I suggested going to the beach. It was a 90-minute drive each way to Biarritz but we'd been landlocked for a couple of months. A carload of us went — Chris, Debbie, Liam and Clark. I'd also told the guys who did my run session that I'd reward them with as much McDonald's as they could eat.

We had the feed and hit the beach. It was just the best day. My session had gone well, it was a hot sunny day and we were body surfing and hanging out. It was just golden, the ultimate day of recovery. To top off my mood, I was washing off the sand at an outdoor shower as we were about to leave when this topless French girl of about 18 walked off the beach and under the shower next to mine. Clark was looking back from the car thinking, 'Man, is that chick topless? Lucky Hamish.'

That night Bevan and Nathan got back from the opening ceremony and were raving about it but I didn't regret not going. Quite the opposite. My past four days had been perfect. I knew I'd gone to a totally new level and I think Bevan could sense that.

My sister, Cath, and her husband, Paul, visited, which added to my already positive morale. It was only a week until we went to the village ourselves. Thankfully, Chris refused to let me do another hard session. I'd recovered quickly from that big session and thought I needed another hard blowout. I argued with him for an entire day but he insisted that I was ready. He told me to be patient. I told him he was wrong and tried to rationalise it, but he wouldn't budge.

I didn't fret. I decided to trust him. I got on the plane rapt with how my training in Pau had gone. I knew I was in the best shape of my life.

THE ESSENTIAL CRISIS

We were the last of the New Zealand team to arrive at the village. I'd decided to put up a wall around me because I knew how the Olympics had destroyed me in Sydney and I was determined not to let it happen again. Instead of walking around the village, soaking up the atmosphere, I tried to shut it all out. Of course, that was the wrong thing to do.

It's very hard to settle in because everything is so foreign. The food hall is the size of Eden Park. You walk 100 m to get a piece of bread, then off somewhere else to get a piece of lettuce. Making a sandwich takes about 20 minutes. You're given a huge bag of new team clothes to wear, and every time you put something on, you have to take it out of the packaging. There was wrapping paper all over the damned room.

Inevitably, at the Olympics, everything seems to get stuffed up. Our bikes were delayed and there was some muck-up with Bevan's room. The day we arrived, Dave Currie, the Chef de Mission, told us we were required for a little initiation ceremony. Typically, I wasn't keen. I didn't want anyone telling me how I should be thinking. I turned inward, started to get a bit angry and was trying to control the game. That's when things began to unravel. I was uncomfortable with the village environment and just wanted to be left alone to do my race. I almost dug my toes in and refused to go. The ceremony included a Maori welcome where we were each given a pounamu pendant. I walked away feeling uplifted by the experience, but underneath I wasn't good. The bad feelings I associated with Sydney were on the rise.

Roger Mortimer

The pressure was on. Ulmer had won the world championship early in the year and then Docherty won his world championship. It was terrific for Bevan and he's an absolutely top-class athlete. Hamish had raced well at the worlds and in terms of timing his season for Athens, it was ideal. But the fact of the matter was that the game had changed.

For so many years Hamish had been the beacon-carrier for New Zealand triathletes. Craig Watson, Jamie Hunt and Paul Amey had come and gone. None had overtaken him. Hamish had been ranked number one but he had never won the world championship. Then Docherty, his arch-rival, won it at 24. Hamish was 33.

With Sarah, it was different; she and Hamish are good friends and she's in a different sport. But those achievements still raised the bar. Hamish had talked about it his whole career and here were two people who were reasonably close to him who went out and did it. Sponsors want big hitters and Hamish was being left behind. There it was. I honestly felt that for Hamish it was now or never.

On my third day there, a huge buzz ran through the New Zealand camp. Sarah had won the pursuit. She came back to the village and you couldn't help but be caught up in it. When you're waiting to compete, celebrating someone else's success is the hardest thing to do. But, for me, it was more than that. I stood at the very back and watched everyone do the haka, watched the champagne flow. I was pleased for her, but I also felt gutted. Mostly, I felt fear. I thought, 'Oh my God, I am never going to have that. Sarah and I have the same sponsors. It'll be Sarah this, Sarah that, and I'm going to be chopped liver.' Roger will say, 'Sorry Hamish, it's over for you.' I went to bed that night a nervous wreck and hardly slept a wink. An endless procession of anxieties raced through my mind. Do I have the right gears on my bike? Gee, Greg Bennett looks fit. Robbo's a much better runner than I am. Bevan has won just about every race he's entered this year. How am I going to beat these guys? I hope I can finish without stuffing up . . . The next morning I felt exhausted. I was convinced I'd blown it. My confidence was at ground zero.

I had to talk to Marisa immediately and went to the team room to ring on the landline. Normally, it's a cool place to be, with silver ferns, pictures of Olympians such as John Walker and positive quotations plastered all over the walls. I'd put up with the albatross of Sydney hanging around my neck for four years and now the same old demons were haunting me. I felt so defeated and must have been as white as a sheet because Michelle Tapper, who ran the desk, asked if I was okay. I lied and told her I was fine. But I was choking up and when I got Marisa on the line, I told her I'd call back. I figured bursting into tears in the team room wouldn't be great for morale. I thought I was having a nervous breakdown; I just felt utterly lost.

I got away from the New Zealand team area — away from where anyone might recognise me — and called Marisa back on my mobile. As soon as I heard her voice, I lost it. I was bawling so much I couldn't speak. There was Marisa, at home in wintry Auckland with a baby and a three-year-old, and a husband on the phone who was totally beside himself. 'What's the matter?' she asked. 'What are you doing?'

I managed to say something like, 'It's too big. I can't do it,' and Marisa blurted out, 'What have you gone and done, had an affair or something?' It was such a Marisa thing to say. It was like a circuit-breaker and I cracked up laughing. Then she let me have it. 'For God's sake, pull yourself together,' she said. 'You're at the Olympic Games. I trained my whole life trying to get there and didn't make it. Now you're there and you're all upset and complaining. I'm at home and it's raining, and you've been away for two months. I refuse to let this be a waste of time. Stop thinking about all this crap that doesn't matter. Whatever happens, you have two great kids and we have a fantastic life. Just enjoy it.' She really blew up at me and it was like a light switching on.

I realised that I might lose the race, but I saw it for what it was. Just a race. I had wanted it so much that it had become a kind of prison. It was almost as though I had to let the race go in my mind to have a chance to win. Otherwise, the pressure of the Olympics would have consumed me. I reckon 80 per cent of athletes don't actually enjoy it or perform as well as they should. You put absolutely everything into it and can't understand what goes wrong. Few people have the confidence to let go — to recognise it's beyond their control and accept that what will be, will be.

After I got off the phone, I stayed sitting where I was and, for the first time, properly looked at the village around me, at the flags with the rings, and thought, 'I'm at the Olympic Games and I'll never be here again. Damn it, I'm going to have a good time and I don't care what happens in the race.' I knew that when the gun went, I would fight to the death. I knew I was in the shape of my life and that all I needed to do now was get to the start line in some sort of positive frame of mind.

I knew my fitness was exceptional, but in my besieged state of mind that had scared me too, because it meant that I could potentially win. That spun me off thinking about the result. And thinking about the result freaked me out. What if someone got away on the bike? What if I had a bad swim and missed the lead group? And, scariest of all, what if the race went perfectly according to plan and I simply wasn't good enough?

It was as though Marisa had lifted a veil from my eyes. I felt lighter, 100 times more positive. I started to meet people's eyes, talk to them and enjoy the Olympic experience. I found Dave Currie and thanked him for persuading me to go to the welcome and told him how I wished I'd been in a frame of mind to remember it more clearly.

On my last night in the village I saw Sarah in the food hall. She asked how I was doing. I said, 'You know what? I was pretty bad, but now I'm good.'

'Dude,' she said, 'just go and enjoy it.'

Day by day, I felt calmer and calmer. Even the race briefing was good for me, two days before the event. All the athletes who had aimed their lives at this race were corralled into one room. I looked around at all the intense faces and realised not one of them was happy. I gained a quiet confidence from that. No one understood what the Olympics were about. It had taken time, but I'd finally got it: the Olympic Games were a load of bullshit, a load of hype. It was just a race, a triathlon. I reminded myself that I'd been doing them for 12 years and that I was pretty good at them. I let go of all those negative feelings and told myself to imagine I was going down to St Heliers to do a local race and have a whole lot of fun. From that moment on, I don't think anything could have upset my state of mind. Right then, that's where I started to win the race.

I knew I'd be alright when I wasn't thrown by Nathan Richmond's decision to break an agreement to help me in the race as payback for me helping him get his spot on the team. I'd blocked for him and slowed the chase after he got away during the bike leg of the last selection race. That gave him a chance to start the run with a big lead, and as a result, he'd been selected to join Bevan and me in Athens.

We'd made a deal that he would race the Olympics for me. As it turned out, he wasn't going well enough to help during the bike leg, but he could have been a big help in the swim. He's a good swimmer and the idea had been for him to pick a start position on the pontoon near me. Even if I hadn't been able to position myself to swim on his feet, having a strong swimmer on my side of the pack could have made it the favoured side. When Nathan picked a spot on the pontoon that wasn't at my end, I realised he was going to do his own race. I was a bit annoyed and thought about speaking to Chris, but there wasn't any point because you can't change your pontoon position. Part of me was pleased for Nathan, but I was also disappointed because we'd had a deal. I'd flown to Tasmania after qualifying for Athens specifically to help Nathan make the team. I wouldn't do it again. If I were to work for someone again, it would probably be for Gemmell, to right a wrong if you like, because he was probably the form athlete of the two.

Later, I discovered my near-breakdown wasn't that uncommon.

On the plane trip home, Sarah and sailboarder Barbara Kendall both said they had meltdowns before their big successes. It's like releasing a pressure valve, letting all your fears and anxieties pour out. I had to literally crack . . . had to have that bollocking from Marisa to be able to see things clearly for what they were. It was one of her finest moments.

The night before the race, I stayed with Nathan, Bevan and the coaches Chris and Mark Elliott in an apartment overlooking the finish at Vouliagmeni Beach, on a beautiful piece of coast. I was enjoying being there.

Chris Pilone

The apartment had three bedrooms. The boys had one each, and Mark and I slept on the couches. I watched television, the women's pole vault I think, until I drifted off to sleep about 1 a.m. I was satisfied that Carter was as fit as he could be.

I didn't know that he'd had a bit of a sob to Marisa. He told me the day before the race that he'd spoken to her and to Sarah, and told me he was just going to go out and enjoy the race tomorrow. I thought to myself, 'He doesn't know.' He knew he was going to race well, but he didn't know he was going to win.

I said, 'That's good, Hamish. When you're in that frame of mind, you make the right decisions. It'll be good.' His face lit up.

That was it as far as he and I discussing the race went. It was funny, because after that bike-run session, I sensed an expectation from him that I was going to tell him how I thought he was going to go, whether he would get a medal. I decided not to say anything, and I got more and more stubborn about that.

That evening, I jumped in the van to go to the delicatessen to pick up a few things we needed for dinner. The deli is right next to the race venue. I don't know why, but I wandered in. It was a lovely warm Greek evening, about 7 p.m., the bikes were racked up in glinting rows and there was nobody there except for one security guard with an AK 47. I walked over to the podium that was set up ready for the medal ceremony and touched the top step. The guy with the gun gave me a smile, and off I went.

Marisa

I was worried sick when I got off the phone from Hamish. I was tearful on and off for a day or so because I thought it was going to be Sydney all over again. I didn't know he'd had this transformation until he phoned again on the eve of the race. He sounded calm. One of the things he mentioned was how his rowing coach had once told him that sometimes he just tried too hard. I knew then that he was going to be alright.

When I went to bed I looked at photos of my kids, Phoebe and Austin, on my computer. As I looked at Austin, I thought about what Marisa had said. He doesn't care whether I win or lose. Sure, it's the Olympics, but to a little boy it's just some dumb race. All he wants is his dad to come home. I turned out the light. I felt ready.

LET'S HAVE FUN

The morning of the race went smoothly. There was no rushing about as there had been in Sydney, where there was a bit of a panic to sign in on time. I felt good, relaxed. So much so, that a reporter from the *New Zealand Herald* who saw me lolling around in the transition area while other athletes were doing warm-ups or fiddling with their bikes thought he had a scoop. He reckoned I looked far too casual for someone about to chase an Olympic medal and asked Mark Elliott if I was a late scratching. If I looked that laid-back, then it was a good sign.

That sense of calm stayed with me even when I was standing on the pontoon. You wouldn't have believed I was the same person who only three days earlier had been a mess of self-doubt and jangling nerves that threatened to sabotage my second Olympics. I was able to put aside all the pressure and anxiety. In Sydney, I'd been obsessing about winning and was absolutely freaking out as we waited for the starter's gun. Here, it couldn't have been more different. I'd told myself this was going to be the most fun day, and I actually believed it.

I soaked it up. I remember looking around at the other guys.

Everyone looked like scared rabbits. No one met my eye. It was as though they didn't dare, in case it gave their fear away. They withdrew into their shells, trying to hold it together until the gun released us into Oceanida Bay.

I kept reminding myself that whatever was about to happen, it would be okay. I was simply going to enjoy the race for its own sake. I'd got so wound up in Sydney that I couldn't race anywhere near my capability. I wasn't going to let that happen this time. I was just going to let it roll and have fun.

Simon Whitfield, 2000 Olympic champion

I stood beside Hamish on the start line of the Olympics in Sydney, and in Athens too. It was purely by chance. In both races we started on the far left of the field.

In Sydney I looked up to him and was thrilled to be starting beside the world number one. We've talked about how he was standing there feeling under pressure and wishing the race was over, while I was thinking, 'This is going to be a blast . . . hope I don't get eaten by a shark'. In Athens, it was the absolute reverse. He was on the line, excited and ready. He later told me how during the swim he was taking in the scenery, looking at the bottom of the Mediterranean and at a passing cruise ship. I was the one on the starting line wishing that the race was over.

It's all about the pressure of expectation. He was a favourite in Sydney; I was the defending Olympic champion in Athens.

I'd been swimming pretty badly during training because I'd got so skinny through the hard work I'd been doing on the bike and especially with my running. Triathlon is a trade-off between the three disciplines. The faster runners are usually slower swimmers and vice versa. You sacrifice a bit here to gain a bit there.

It's a balancing act and very difficult to get right. You want to be as light and lean as possible to maximise your running, but you need a bit of muscle bulk on your upper body to get the best from your swimming and enough meat on your legs to propel the bike through the wind. Maybe we'd tilted the balance a bit further than we thought away from swimming and in favour of feeling light and fast for the run.

So, although I expected to be in the mix coming out of the water, I wasn't anticipating having a great swim. I also had another problem. Greg Bennett, who started on one side of me, had decided he was going to swim on my wake. If you're not one of the strongest swimmers, you can get an advantage by positioning yourself on someone's hip and swimming on their bow-wave. You get a bit of a tow along but it makes it harder for the swimmer in front because it affects his flow by pushing water back into him. It doesn't matter if someone is drafting off you by swimming on your feet but sitting on your hip, as Greg was doing . . . it's like swimming with a piano on your back.

Usually, I'm one of the best swimmers but obviously Greg hadn't heard about my recent swimming form! I tried to shake him off by accelerating, but couldn't. So I had to make a call, because towing him all the way out to the first buoy could have meant trouble. It can get pretty tight as the field bunches going around the mark. If you're tired from towing someone, you can easily be pushed under. By the time you get going again, you're out the back door.

I slowed right down to force Greg to come off my wake and swim up beside me. We slowed so much that we basically watched the field swim away. By the time we got to the first mark we were worse than mid-pack and that's bad. You can ruin a race by getting into a negative mindset thinking it's all over after just a few hundred metres. There weren't a lot of options — panic or don't panic. 'It doesn't matter,' I told myself. I knew I was going to come out of the water in the back half of the field, because after the first turn on the swim it's very hard to move up through the pack. There was nothing I could do about it and just accepting that was a big thing for me. Relax man, just relax, I kept repeating to myself. And the weird thing was that I actually did. I was even taking in the scenery, noticing what a nice day it was each time I turned my head to take a breath, and thinking how beautifully clean the water was. Stressing out wasn't going to make me go any faster. As it turned out, I was able to move up several places in the last part of the swim as gaps opened in the field.

Commentary

American Andy Potts, a former Olympic swimmer, is first out of the water. Nathan Richmond is best placed of the Kiwis in 11th, 20 seconds behind. Bevan Docherty is a further four seconds back in 17th place. Carter is in 33rd position, 30 seconds behind Potts, something of a surprise, as Carter is usually among the first out of the water.

The transition to the bike is always an intense part of a race, more so on this occasion because most of the bikes were gone when I got there. This transition and the first few kilometres of the cycle were crucial for me because I was so far back in the field. I had to ride up to the front pretty damn smartly. The pace was on and I knew I had to absolutely smoke it up the hill the first time because if a break went away on that first lap without me, that could be the whole race. I was lucky that the first few guys didn't put the hammer down hard as soon as they got on their bikes, which might have forced a gap that would prove to be the decisive move.

Thankfully, when I started climbing I seemed to be moving past people easily even though I was really hurting. I didn't yet have my riding legs. Blood was still migrating from my shoulders, where it was needed for the swim, to my leg muscles, which were screaming for more oxygen. By the time I got to the crest of the hill I could see the front of the race. That was a hell of a relief because my poor swim had left me very vulnerable. 'Okay, stay calm,' I thought. 'I've had a bad swim but I've managed to get away with it.'

Chris Pilone

The one mistake that Mark [Elliott] and I made was not having swimming expertise in the camp at Pau. That was a major stuff-up. If there'd been a split among the leaders as they transitioned to the bike, Hamish might have had to work bloody hard to catch them. We weren't too worried though. We watched the swim from the grandstand and could see that they had come out in one continuous line. There were no real gaps in the field that could have made it really dangerous. Mark and I then walked two-thirds of the way up the climb and watched the cycle from there.

Commentary

Docherty leads over the summit followed by Simon Thompson of Australia, and powerful Swiss cyclist Olivier Marceau, who has quickly moved up after a moderate swim. Australian Peter Robertson, a three-time world champion, is handy. Carter has moved up 19 places in the first few kilometres and goes over in 14th position.

By the end of the first of five 8 km laps, Docherty and Carter are in the leading group of 15. Twenty seconds behind is a bunch containing several favoured contenders, including former world champions Ivan Rana (Spain) and Dmitriy Gaag (Kazakhstan), Thompson, who crashed when in the leading group, in-form American Hunter Kemper and Whitfield, the Olympic and Commonwealth champion.

That hill was steep and gnarly, and we knew it was going to be a factor. We also thought it could suit our strength-based style of racing, so long as we prepared well for it. And we had, particularly at our training camp in Pau. There, the Pyrenees were on our doorstep. Some of the Pyrenean passes are famous from the Tour de France, which includes these mountains on the French–Spanish border in its route each year. We'd found a hill there that was much steeper than this one in Athens and used it for my hill repetition workouts. I've always been able to climb, but I'm sure that that training helped me immensely.

The hill in Athens was one of the toughest ever included in a top-level triathlon. In the women's race particularly, some competitors snaked their way up the steepest sections, zig-zagging from one side of the road to the other.

Five ascents made it a true test of cycling strength. Adding to the uncertainty was the fact that it was a virgin course. We'd ridden it in training, but no one had raced on it.

The big question was going to be how much damage it would do, especially to the pure runners who, on easier courses, can hide in the bunch, expending minimal energy and then run like startled hares. Would any of them still be in touch when we jumped off our bikes? And what toll would the hard cycle take on the running legs of those still in the hunt?

Commentary

Robertson charges into the hill the second time, trying to set up a breakaway with Marceau. This time Docherty accelerates after them, as does another Swiss, Sven Riederer, and Carter. The order over the top the second time is: Docherty, Carter, Robertson, Marceau, Riederer. The steepness of the climb and 30-degree temperature are already taking a toll. The five get a small gap but the front bunch reforms on the descent and still numbers 15 at the end of the second lap. The next group is 28 seconds back.

On the first two laps of the ride, some of the guys attacked on the hill and some surged off the front on the flat part of the circuit. Robbo [Robertson] had a dab on the climb in the early laps, along with one or two who weren't great runners so needed to hammer on the bike. Marceau was in that category. He's one of the tough guys on the bike and is always looking for an opportunity to get a break or wear down the quicker runners. Robbo can run with the best on his day and by nature likes to attack. Being aggressive on the bike has paid off for him before. He won the world championship in 2003 after riding away with Marceau. These are guys you have to keep your eye on.

I was feeling good, starting to relax and enjoy the race. I looked to see who was with me in the front group and was taking in information about the course. How windy is it here at the bottom turn? How hot does it feel? I was trying to gauge how the hill was going to affect my legs. Because of the training I'd done on that brute of a climb near Pau, this one didn't seem so bad. As I went up the second time, it seemed much easier than I'd anticipated.

Things became settled after the second ascent. No one attacked on the flat any more. The climb had become such a factor that everyone felt they had to conserve energy for it. If they used too much gas bursting off the front on the flat, they risked getting killed on the hill. I felt stronger each time we went up and, equally, I sensed that the others were growing more tired. The hill was blowing the field to bits. With each ascent, guys were getting shelled out the back door. I was surprised. I had thought everyone would have ridden hills all summer in preparation.

Bevan drove the pace for the first part of the cycle. I was sitting back watching, happy for him to do that. I knew it was going to be a war of attrition. Pilone had said as much to me, over and over again. He'd told me not to attack, that there would be a lot of gung-ho athletes wanting to rip into it. But it's a race that takes an hour and 50 minutes. Our plan was to conserve energy whenever I could and be confident that the demands of the course would take their toll. I could understand why Bevan was working on the front of the group so much early on. He was probably like I was in Sydney. The hardest thing for an athlete, particularly when you're on form or have great expectations, is to be patient and ride easy.

Marisa

I'd felt pretty nervous during the day of the race. It was on at 7 p.m. New Zealand time, showing live on television. I tried to keep busy. It was my nephew's birthday, so that occupied me for a while. I went to the gym and, later, for a run along the waterfront. I stopped under the Auckland Harbour Bridge. It was a beautiful day and I watched the yachts and looked back at the high-rises of the city and up at the sky. I said a silent prayer: 'If someone is out there, please make him win!'

Watching him race is just the worst thing. You can't do anything to help. At least when you're competing yourself, the gun goes and your nerves disappear as you get absorbed in the process of racing. My parents and some friends, Tracy and Carla, came over. Mum and Dad brought dinner but I could hardly eat a thing. I felt sick. That wasn't helped by the swim. It's unusual for Hamish to be that far back.

But I saw him at the top of the hill, and then the second time up I just knew he was feeling good. Even though he wasn't on the front, I wasn't anxious any more. At one point I saw Bevan shout at someone, to get them to work. Hamish would have done that four years ago. Now he'd just sit quietly in the group. So I knew where Bevan was at and where Hamish was at, and I was feeling quite good about it.

Commentary

Marceau is hard at work and Docherty is prominent as they climb the hill for the third time. Carter rides in the saddle, his upper body still, the others ride out off the seat rocking their bodies from side to side with each turn of the pedals. The Kiwis and the two Swiss lead over the top, followed by Englishman Andrew Johns. France's Frederic Belaubre makes a rapid descent to complete a leading group of six while Greg Bennett, one of the favoured Australian trio, is just a few lengths adrift over the top of the hill.

I was playing a little game with myself. On the hill, I'd stay in the saddle long after everyone else stood up on the pedals. I guess it was a psychological ploy. I was thinking, 'I'm riding great. I can climb this hill in the saddle while everyone else has to stand up.' I'd get out of the saddle over the crest, but because I'd stood up so much later than the others, it was easy for me to accelerate over the top. It was still hard work but I was looking forward to the hill each lap. Bit by bit I felt I was gaining control of the race.

Olivier kept the pace on as we descended on the third lap. The rest of us immediately began to work, rolling through to take turns punching into the wind at the front because we sensed an opportunity. Six of us got a small gap. I can't recall whether much was said but the mood was 'Let's move it, we've got a nice compact group here'.

The most efficient way for a group like this to ride is for everyone to take short turns at the front. Viewed from above, the bunch is shaped like a sausage, with the riders in two constantly rotating lines. One line moves forwards and the other back. You follow the back wheel of the rider immediately ahead until he reaches the front and moves over to the head of the retreating line. You follow suit, as does the rider trailing you. What it means is that you're always riding in a slipstream, except for the 15 or so seconds you spend on the front facing the wind.

As we were revolving around like this, AJ, the English athlete Andrew Johns, accidentally clipped my rear wheel with his front wheel. There was a big rub and then a flick as the wheels touched then separated. Your heart goes into your mouth. We just looked at each other. I said, 'Take it easy, man,' and he said, 'Yeah, sorry.' It was almost funny, but it wasn't. The last thing we wanted was to take each other out with a silly crash.

AJ was potentially the fastest runner in the group and so I'd normally be concerned about him being in the break. Some of the guys, including Bevan, were yelling at him to work harder. They were wary that AJ might be faking, taking soft turns to save his energy for the run. We needed to make sure that everyone was doing their share of the workload. Otherwise, if you tow someone around, they'll come off the bike as fresh as a daisy. AJ copped some flak, but I think he was doing as much as he could because the ride certainly took a toll on him. It was a super-honest group. Everyone did what they could to help us pull away from the chasers.

There were three world champions in the breakaway group: Bevan, the reigning champ, Marceau, who won in 2000, and Fred Belaubre, a former junior champion. Belaubre is phenomenally strong for his age. I was impressed by how he climbed the hill and hung with us in such a tough race. If there were any surprises among the six it may have been Fred, because of his age, or AJ, who is better known for his running than biking. It wasn't the sort of breakaway that you might get into through luck, say when the bunch chooses not to chase a move. It was a case of the six strongest on the climb dropping the rest.

I wasn't thinking about the personalities in the group so much as watching for signs of fatigue and checking whether everyone was contributing. I was also in a state of disbelief that our small group had got away. Six is an ideal number for a breakaway, enough to give you a good rest as you roll off the front after doing your lap, and enough to put some time on the chasing group. It's also a manageable number. If you have 10 riders, there are always one or two trying to shirk at the back. When a breakaway carries a passenger, everyone else is reluctant to put in too much effort so the whole group slows.

At the point on the course where we turned around a marker to double back, we saw that we had a good lead. But there were three more laps, three more ascents and, no matter how big your lead, if you've worked too hard for it, you pay the price during the run. The run was still going to be the winning of the race. I was confident of running well. I was the lightest I'd been, 67 or 68 kg. That's why I had swum so badly. When you're really skinny, you just sink.

Marisa

I hadn't seen Hamish for more than a month, since he went overseas on the final stage of his preparation for the race, and I was struck by how skinny he looked. His ribs were sticking out.

He was taking regular drinks, which was good. It showed that he was relaxed, because if you're stressed or struggling with the pace, that's the first thing you forget and it can cost you later, especially on such hot days.

Commentary

Carter leads over the crest on lap four. Kris Gemmell, guest commentator for Television New Zealand: 'In the last four weeks at the camp in the South of France, I did a few rides with Hame. He was very confident on the climbs and as you can see now, it looks like he's dancing up them.'

The two Kiwis are emerging as the strongest riders. It's expected that Marceau will attack the final time up the climb but he appears unable to make the charge and Carter leads Docherty over the summit, followed by the other four with Johns fighting to maintain contact.

By the last lap of the cycle no one was yelling at AJ to take bigger turns any more. He was obviously struggling. Bad for him, but for the rest of us it was good to see that at least one of the six was on the ropes. I think we were all feeling it the last time up the climb. You almost had to attack it to get sufficient momentum, because if you tried to take it more easily you would nearly stall.

Sven Riederer was climbing strongly. I didn't know him that well. He and Belaubre surprised me because I wasn't sure of their capabilities. Marceau had been in the sport about as long as I had and was always strong on the bike. Even though he wasn't renowned as a fast runner, in a true triathlon like this, where no one would get to the run unscathed, nothing could be assumed. After all, Marceau had won his world title by out-running a small breakaway group.

It was as though everything that had happened up to this point was in the past. Reputations and previous results counted for nothing. I was concentrating on staying relaxed. I was reasonably confident I'd got through the ride in good shape. Bevan had been stretching his back, which can be an indication of soreness or fatigue. But until you put your running shoes on, you just don't know. If you're battling, you may be able to disguise it on the bike, but once the run starts there's nowhere to hide.

As we approached the transition, I slipped my feet out of my cycling shoes, which stay clipped onto the pedals. Once in the transition area you run to your allotted spot, rack your bike, remove your helmet, put your running shoes on and go! As I ran off, I saw Bevan having trouble getting his helmet off. That cost him a few metres.

I found myself in front when I cleared the transition area but wasn't tempted to attack. I was running at a good pace and trying to concentrate on finding my rhythm. Going from the bike to the run is such a shock to the body and the first kilometre can be like a wrecker's yard. This was no exception. I got a surprise when I realised that only Bevan and Sven were with me.

I was stoked to be at the front of the race for a change instead of starting the run a minute down as I had in my lead-up races, London and Lifetime Fitness. But I couldn't get too excited. There was a real chance that a big threat would come out of the chasing pack, partly because the quickest runners are not usually the strongest cyclists and also because in a bigger group they are more likely to have got away with a soft ride. I knew we'd got a good break but I didn't know how far behind the chasers were. In fact, we had a lead of 44 seconds on the next group, which included good runners such as Bennett and Robertson. But I wasn't thinking much about what might be happening behind me, or even what was going on around me. I was concentrating on myself. I thought, 'Well, it's been a good race and I'm enjoying it and I'm still feeling good'.

In fact, I felt so comfortable that I decided to push the pace to see what happened. I opened a gap of a couple of metres quite easily but it happened to coincide with the part of the course where Pilone was standing and he called out for me to relax, to wait. I was tempted to have a crack there and then. I felt that I could do it, but it's always a risk with so far to go. If you run hard in the first 5 km it's easy to blow up, especially in the heat, and quickly go from hero to zero.

I know Bevan's style. He loves to race from the front, so when I buttoned off the pace and he didn't immediately come through to lead, I realised he must be tired. I backed off a bit more because I wanted them to come past so I could see how they were moving. Sven looked fatigued but I wasn't so sure about Bevan.

Commentary

At the end of the first of three laps, the trio are 28 seconds ahead of the fading Belaubre and Marceau. Johns has blown completely. Bennett is next, running alone. He's chipped back nine seconds and is 35 seconds from the leaders. TVNZ commentator Brendan Telfer nominates Bennett as the danger, suggesting that he may run down those who got away on the bike, as had happened in the women's race a day earlier.

Before long I found myself running in front again without making a conscious effort to do so. That gave me a confidence boost because it can be an indication that you are the strongest. It was only then that it dawned on me that I was absolutely on fire. That was an amazing realisation but it was also scary. I was afraid of blowing it. Sudden bad patches can take you by surprise, and if you get carried away with how good you feel, the lows are so much harder to fight through.

Bevan had won the world champs in a 100-metre sprint and I wasn't likely to out-kick him in a dash for the line. I couldn't wait forever. I would have to put the pressure on him at some point. But Pilone was right, it was too soon. There was still 7 km to go. Pilone was calling for me to keep the pace steady but not to surge, to grind them down. The race had become a war of attrition; the goal was to be last man standing.

I kept telling myself that there is no prize for being in front at the 5 km mark. Assumptions can be dangerous, too. I've been in races before when I've thought I had everyone covered and then someone attacked and I couldn't go with them. At this late stage of a race, even a small increase in speed can have a devastating effect and you never know whether someone has more gas in the tank than they appear to. After all, it's the Olympics and Bevan is a fierce competitor.

I was also aware that Greg Bennett was gaining — another reason to keep the pace high. I didn't want four people in our front group. I was hedging my bets, pushing it along, but not trying to make a winning break.

Greg Bennett

Because Loretta Harrop had been run down by Kate Allen from the chasing bunch the day before, there was an expectation in the Australian camp that I was going to do the same. It was quite the show. I was doing the math. When they yelled out that it was 40 seconds to the leaders, I thought, 'Okay, four seconds a k'. At five kilometres I was on target but I was absolutely sprinting. When I got to six kilometres, seven kilometres, all of a sudden that gap wasn't coming back as quick as I needed and that's when it became real tough. I think you can see it on the television replay. Although I'm still running fast, the quads are starting to cramp. I was just waiting for Sven Riederer to drop off, because I wasn't racing for the gold once I got to about eight kilometres. I knew Hamish and Bevan were going to be the toughest guys to take 20 seconds off in two kilometres, and then beat them in a sprint.

On the third and last lap, the pace eased. I knew Greg wasn't going to catch us. It was down to three. That's a nervous time. Unless you're really struggling, it's when you start thinking about when to play your cards. Bevan was first to make a move but it wasn't earth-shattering. He put in a surge — a tester, I think — to see how we'd respond. I still felt good and Sven stuck with us.

Heading out to the last turn we ran up to a Mexican competitor who was a lap behind. Unnoticed by me, he hooked in behind us. When I realised there was a fourth person there I got a hell of a shock. For a split second I thought, 'Holy shit, it's Greg'.

I went to the back and had a good look at Bevan and Sven. Sven was at his maximum, his head rolling with the effort. I knew that he was history. It was Bevan or me.

TWO MINUTES THAT CHANGED MY LIFE

Bevan was driving the pace and I had the impression that he was worried about Greg possibly catching us. He looked a bit laboured in the way he was carrying his shoulders and it crossed my mind that his focus may have shifted a little from winning to making sure he got a medal. I was certain we weren't going to be caught, but I was trying to stay super aware, ready for any move, because something had to happen soon.

Marisa

When it became clear that they weren't going to be caught, I knew Hamish would beat Bevan. Nothing against Bevan; I just thought he'd be happy with second and I knew Hamish wouldn't. There was no way, having got this far, that he'd settle for a silver medal or being second New Zealander. It was Bevan's first Olympics and he'd had a great year. For Hamish, this was it.

As we turned around the cone for the last time, with a kilometre to go, Bevan ran hard out of the corner because he could see that Sven was at the end of his tether. We began to move clear and Bevan said, 'We've dropped him.' That told me Bevan was thinking about second, that he had the silver sewn up. It was a chink in his armour. I didn't say anything, I didn't even glance at him. This was my chance; I attacked him immediately.

He matched strides with me for 50 metres or so, then I couldn't see him any more out of the corner of my eye or hear his breathing. I was in a world of hurt but sensed I was pulling away. I had to keep a tiny bit in the tank, because if he came back at me, I'd need to go again. I was preparing myself mentally for that so it was a bit of a surprise when I took a quick look around and saw the gap that had opened up. 'Right,' I told myself, 'give it everything!'

On the last bend, I noticed there were a few Australian flags and none of them were waving! The Aussies are a pretty cocky lot and had expected to dominate. A few seconds later I rounded the bend and saw the finish tape. That's when it really hit me: 'Crikey, I'm going to win!' I had about 50 metres to enjoy it. It was unreal; I couldn't really believe it was happening. I resisted the temptation to veer over to where someone in the crowd was waving a New Zealand flag, in case I tripped over the legs of the crowd-control barriers, and then I ran through the tape and collapsed in a heap. Bloody hell, I'd done it!

As I lay there sprawled on the ground, the first voice I heard was that of ITU official Leslie Beckerman as she tried to pull me to my feet. 'You can't fall over,' she said. 'It looks terrible for the sport.'

'Who cares?' I told her. 'I just won!' I was euphoric and everything seemed quite surreal. The temperature was in the 30s and there she was wearing this ridiculous uniform, a big double-breasted jacket, big hat and long trousers. I remember telling her she must be really hot. Trevor Mallard, New Zealand's Minister of Sport and Recreation, was behind the partition beside the finish. New Zealand had just finished first and second and Mallard had a look of total disbelief on his face. I gave him a hug and he was sweating more than I was.

I was told off for upsetting the pecking order for media interviews, too. I'd spotted Andrew Saville, from Radio New Zealand, leaning over the barrier and went over and talked to him until another official dragged me away for breaking the media protocol. Apparently, I was supposed to speak to NBC first, then someone else, all in the right order. These officials kept jumping on me, telling me that I was doing everything wrong. I just wanted to talk to the New Zealand media and was thinking, 'Give me a break, man, I've just won the Olympic Games triathlon!'

I was fizzing so much, I could hardly get my head around what had just happened. I'd concentrated so hard on methodically breaking down everything I needed to do in the race that I hadn't thought about winning, or even really allowed it to penetrate my consciousness that this was the Olympics. Suddenly it was over and I was being swept along in some mad, chaotic dream.

Brendan Telfer, TVNZ sports commentator

Gold medal for Carter. It hasn't finished yet. Silver medal for Docherty. New Zealand one and two in the triathlon. The closest New Zealand has come to this in a single race in the 108-year history of the Olympics is Tokyo 1964, gold and bronze in the 1500 metres. Well, this surpasses the performances of Peter Snell and John Davies. This is one of the greatest days in the history of New Zealand at the Olympic Games, up there with Rome 1960 when Peter Snell and Murray Halberg won gold in the 800 and 5000 metre races. The phrase 'Carter and Docherty' has just been added to the sporting lexicon along with Snell and Halberg. In decades to come we'll be talking about this day.

It's special to watch him come back from the depths of despair in Sydney four long years ago. At 33 years of age it was Athens or the bush today and he's come through in the twilight of his career with a truly wonderful victory. In the end, they couldn't get Carter, the man who seems to have a permanent smile on his face. I imagine it will never leave him now.

He was right, it was my dream race, my dream result and the dream way to cap a career. Because of my poor swim, it wasn't the perfect race. But from the first lap on the bike, it couldn't possibly have gone better. To win and to have another Kiwi, the world champion, take the silver . . . Well, you can't ask for more. From the moment that I attacked Bevan to the moment that I broke the finishing tape took a fraction less than two minutes — two minutes that changed my life.

All the journalists wanted to know how I felt about Sydney now.

It had been like a wound and now I could honestly say that it had healed. Not that I'll ever forget it. It drove me on, and without that failure, and having to learn and grow from it, I don't think Athens would have happened for me. I felt as though I'd finally buried the ghost of Sydney. When Australia's 400 metre Olympic champion, Cathy Freeman, carried enormous home expectation to win gold, I remember her saying after her victory that her overwhelming emotion was relief. Mine was joy, pure joy.

Riederer held on for the bronze, with Bennett fourth. Belaubre, in fifth, ran the length of the finishing chute's blue carpet waving to the crowd. Riederer, who looked as if he'd died and gone to heaven, did an elaborate bow to the Swiss fans. He'd had a blinder, a race that not even he would have anticipated. Bevan was ecstatic too. We were stoked to have finished one-two for New Zealand — but I know that if the order had been reversed I would have been devastated and angry, because it was my race to win and I'd have felt as if I had blown it. I couldn't have banked on coming back for another shot.

In Sydney I'd been literally in the gutter, distraught and depressed. Here I was four years later, utterly elated, when all around me were athletes who were feeling gutted and that they had failed. The Olympics is a brutal, vicious environment. The highest highs are within your reach, but also the lowest lows. So it meant a lot to me that good friends who were in the race were genuinely pleased for me, despite their own disappointment. Simon [Whitfield], Greg [Bennett] and Olivier Marceau all made the effort to come over and tell me how pleased they were that I'd won; that I deserved it. Having that recognition from peers I respect was so precious and it says a lot about them as people. Saying 'Awesome, man' to someone who's just achieved what you dreamed of, and failed to achieve, is a hard thing to do. Simon gave me a hug. When he won in Sydney, I regret that I was in such a low place that I wasn't able to do that for him.

Simon Whitfield,

11th, 2 min 08 sec behind Carter

There's a point on the run where the course loops back on itself. As I was heading out, I saw the leaders coming back. They were inside the last kilometre and Hamish had a small gap on Bevan. It's ridiculous, because I should have been focused on my own race, but I yelled across the road to Hamish, calling for him to win. No disrespect to Bevan but the honest truth was that Hamish had played bridesmaid for a while. Both Greg Bennett and I were ecstatic because it was time for Hamish to win the big one. If it couldn't have been us, we wanted it to be him.

I had a terrible swim and hesitated on the bike, which cost me everything. By the time I caught the main group, Hamish and the others had already gone. Then when Greg attacked and gave chase I didn't go with him. Split-second decisions are viewed in the light of how the race turns out. I lost, so people will say that I hesitated and perhaps didn't have the strength. But had the breakaway been pulled back and I'd come through, it would have been seen as a brilliant tactical decision. But Hamish and Bevan put themselves in the driver's seat. There were no variables, no hoping the lead group would come back. They drove right off the front and won the race.

Bevan was the favourite. He was on such a roll and handled the pressure so well to go into that race as world champion and pull out a second. The difference between first and second is minuscule and if I'd had to bet which of the two would take gold, I would have sat on the fence like every good Canadian. But I wasn't surprised Hamish won. I think it was meant to happen for him that day.

Greg Bennett,

fourth, 8 sec from bronze, 34 sec behind Carter

A medal for a mate is something special. We all commit so much to be the best in the world and Hamish deserved it. We've been around a long time and done something like 13 world championships; he and I are the elder statesmen. There are very few guys in the sport about whom I can say, with no bullshit, that I want the best for him.

Bevan is a mate too. As much as the Aussies and Kiwis are rivals, we hang out together on the triathlon circuit. It's like they're our younger brothers. You're always fighting and you want to beat them, but when you take on the neighbourhood kids — or the rest of the world — you unite. You're brothers in arms. Our relationship is like that.

I know how hard Hamish and Bevan worked for it, and if you're going to be beaten, you want it to be by tough bastards. Athens was one of the toughest triathlons I've done. There hasn't been a course like it. It was beautiful, but very demanding. People don't appreciate how hard that climb was. Cyclists will understand when I say that I used my 27 sprocket. Riders who were over-geared had to zig-zag to get up it. But it wasn't only the hill. After that you were into the big gears, slogging out to the turn and all the way back. The run became a pure test of strength and endurance, something our sport hasn't seen for so long, and that's why so many so-called world champions were blown out the back door. Those guys were minutes back. They were used to running a fast 10 km but at Athens if you couldn't get up near the front, if you couldn't bike — not just technically well, but with superior fitness and strength — and then get off and run strongly, you were gone.

The result was no surprise. You had Hamish, the old guard who's as strong as hell, and Bevan, the new kid on the block, the world champion that year and the in-form athlete. Sven was the bolter. He's a good bike rider and pulled out his greatest race. It wasn't as though the chasing pack didn't work together during the bike. We all tried.

I was hoping Sven would fade enough during the run for me to catch him but that was only going to happen if Hamish and Bevan attacked with 3 km to go instead of one. I'd have loved to have been on the podium with those guys, but at the same time, I had a great race. The Australian media was pretty good to me, even though I didn't get a medal. They enjoyed the show and could see that I'd given everything.

I had no idea that it was the first time in athletics since Tokyo that two New Zealanders had won Olympic medals in the same race. I was so inwardly focused right up until the end of the race that I didn't even know it was live on television in New Zealand or even what time it was back home. I'd assumed that it would be the middle of the night. Marisa figured that I didn't need the pressure of knowing all these people in New Zealand, all my friends and family, would be watching, and she was so right. I rang home within 10 minutes of crossing the line, before the medal presentation, and thought I'd have to wake Marisa to tell her the news. It never entered my head that there might be a party going on at my house.

The officials were trying to keep to a timetable, corralling us and getting us organised for the ceremony. I was hunting around for my tracksuit jacket, which I was supposed to wear to receive my medal, and I found the bag with my cellphone in it. I grabbed it and called Marisa from behind the grandstand, but I had to be quick because the presentation was about to start. When I hung up, an official took my phone because they were banned during the ceremony. That was the last I saw of it for a couple of days.

Marisa

My mother said it was meant to be. It was the 28th Olympiad, both Hamish and I were born on the 28th and Hamish wore number 28.

All the local media descended on our doorstep. Hilton Brown, my ex-swim coach, Rick Wells and the neighbours came over. Everyone brought champagne. There was a lot of noise and Phoebe, who was five months old, started screaming. Austin was the only one asleep in the house and if you know Austin, you don't wake him up. The phone was going crazy. Friends had been ringing since Hamish got into the front group on the bike.

And then, next thing Hamish was on the phone yelling, 'I won! I won!' and I was saying, 'I know, I know, I saw!' I felt utter relief. That's the only way I can describe it. We didn't have to worry any more. I'd cried watching Sarah Ulmer being presented with her medal but not during Hamish's medal ceremony. As I watched Sarah, I wanted that so much for Hamish, and when he won, I just felt relief. Hamish had to get off the phone for the medal presentation. As soon as I hung up, it rang again. It was Roger. He was a blubbering mess.

As we walked out for the presentation, Dave Currie and some of the Kiwi contingent did a haka, which was so cool because at that point I was feeling a bit alone. Marisa wasn't there and I had no family there. I'd just done interview after interview. Then I'd been rushing around trying to find my tracksuit and going through the protocol for the march out

Delly Carr/Sportshoot

World Championships in Japan, 2005. I finished 4th.

Carter Collection

The life of a professional athlete is not all glamour! Sleeping in the back of some bus, somewhere . . .

Carter Collection

Good times. Out with the boys after the Queenstown World Champs. Roger, standing, was always working. The others are, from left, Gog, Cameron Brown and Mark Watson.

Carter Collection

Looking the part wearing our compulsory kimonos, at a New Zealand team function at the World Champs in Japan, 2005.

Carter Collection

More good times. This time with Laura and Greg Bennett.

Carter Collection

Out for dinner while at the Olympic camp in Pau, France, 2004. The looks on our faces say it all! Clockwise: Dale Warrender, grumpy me, Bevan Docherty, Nathan Richmond, Clark Ellis and Chris Pilone.

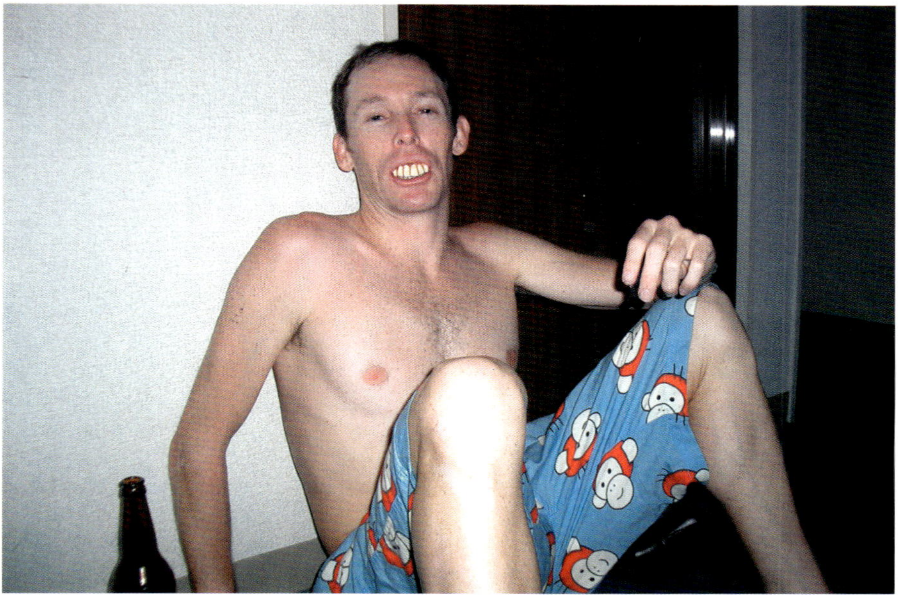

Carter Collection

Great mate Chris Hill and his fabulous teeth, in a Japanese hotel.

Carter Collection

The start of the Edmonton World Championships in 2001. I was racing with a torn Achilles tendon.

Carter Collection

Emma Snowsill and Greg Bennett doing something triathletes can't usually do — drink. Emma is taking a gulp before passing it on!

Carter Collection

New Zealand 2004 Olympic team — killing time waiting for yet another plane. From left, Bevan Docherty, Nathan Richmond and me.

Carter Collection

Sister Cath and her family paid a visit while we were in Pau in 2004. From left: Theo, Zarina, me, Rousseau, Cath and Paul.

Carter Collection

This time they got to come along — Marisa, Phoebe and Austin en route to Victoria, Canada, 2005.

Carter Collection

Bevan Docherty, Simon Whitfield and me in Times Square, New York, 2002.

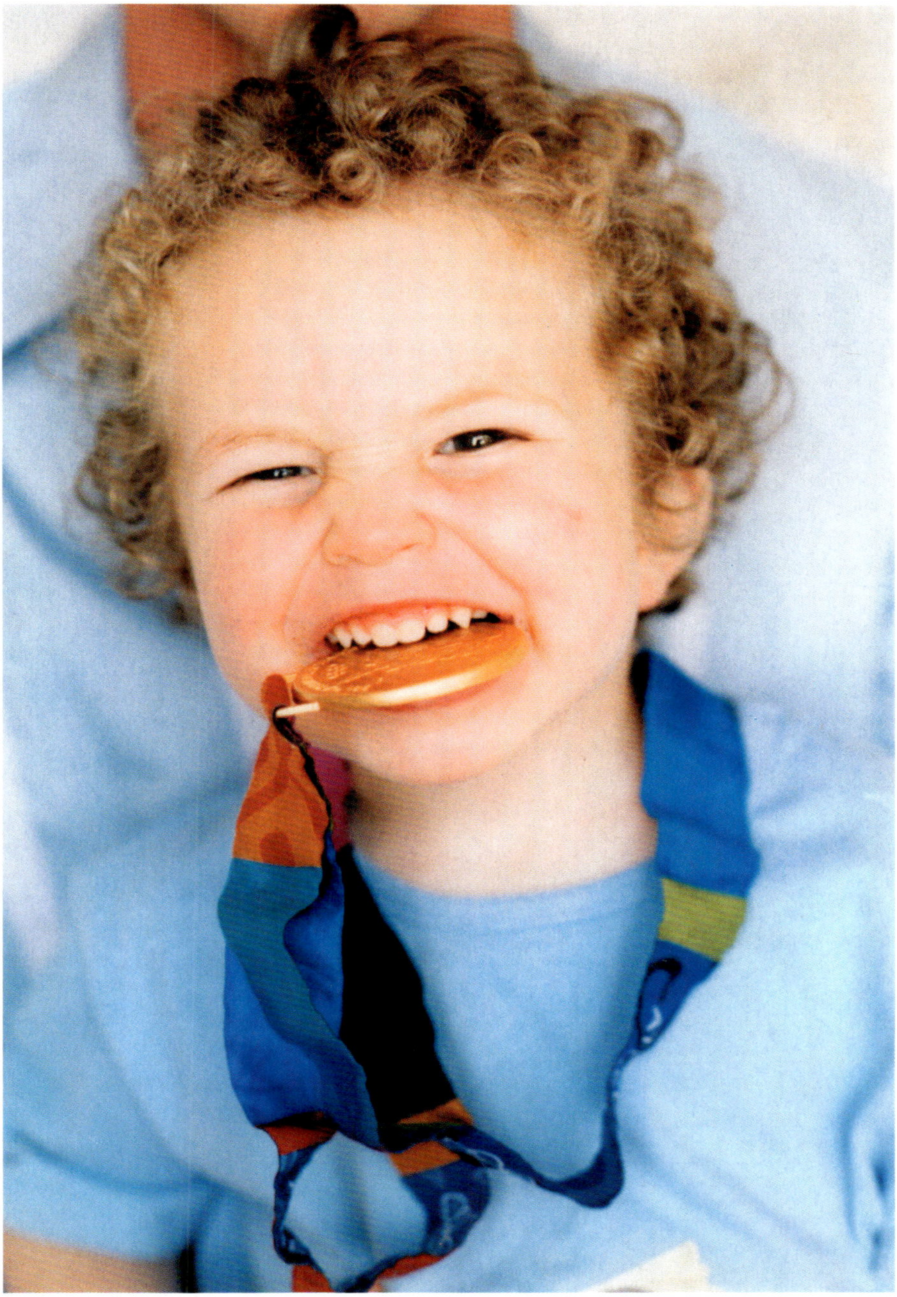

Carter Collection

Austin checking out the quality of the gold in my Olympic medal.

Photosport

Draped in the New Zealand flag, holding that elusive medal, and one big grin. Shortly after the medal ceremony in Athens, 26 August, 2004.

Carter Collection

Rog and I sign off. Departing after my final race as a pro in the Xterra World Champs in 2006.

to the dais. I wanted everything to stop for a minute so that I could take it all in. It was washing over me too fast and I still couldn't believe it was real. The ceremony is such a blur, but I know that there were a lot of Kiwis there because I could hear them calling out. Tay Wilson, a New Zealander who's a member of the IOC, presented the medals. I didn't know him then, but do now. He's the man with the crushing handshake. It felt like he'd broken my bloody hand. I guess he must have felt pretty charged too, presenting gold and silver to his countrymen.

I've been through a lot of medal ceremonies but none like this one. I tried to keep my composure and told myself to just stand there and be cool. I felt dizzy, like the world was swirling around me. Then the anthem started and the two New Zealand flags began inching up the flagpoles. I choked up, I couldn't help it. It was pure magic. I could hear the band in one ear and Kiwis in the grandstand singing in the other, half a beat behind the music because of the distance between them. I thought of singing along but decided not to risk it.

Pilone watched the ceremony from in front of the grandstand, squatting down before a sea of cameras. There'd been some cock-up with his official pass but Nathan smuggled him in.

Chris Pilone

When Richmond saw that they wouldn't let me into what they call the mix zone, where the athletes were, he collared some Greek official and said, 'This. Man. Coach. Gold. Medal. Winner.' The Greek guy seemed to speak English fine. He said, 'Right, you come with me,' and grabbed hold of me, with Richmond in tow, and took us under a big bank of television cameras. He told us we could watch the presentation from here, but not to stand up because we'd stuff up the worldwide broadcast. It was bloody funny.

It was great to see the presentation because I didn't see the finish. Mark Elliott, Liam Scopes and I saw Carter and Docherty go past with 600 or 700 metres to go. I found out from a Radio New Zealand reporter that Carter won. I was rapt, but the full meaning of it didn't hit me until weeks later. People say, 'It must have been fantastic', and it was, but I was expectant rather than hopeful of that result, and I was just glad that it was over.

I got to speak to Hamish after the presentation and the first thing he said was, 'Well, you got that right Pilone,' in reference to our debates about his training in which I'd stuck to my guns when Hamish wanted to make changes.

It was interesting to hear Hamish talking to the press about Sydney. I said to him, 'That Sydney thing, it pissed you off a bit didn't it?' He fixed me with a stare, a glare almost, and said, 'Yes, it did.' And this is just after he's been crowned Olympic champion. I hadn't fully appreciated how deeply Sydney had affected him. I think that helped fuel him in Athens. Sometimes an athlete has something inside them that you didn't know they had. That's how he was on that day, the way he raced. You can't coach that.

In the mix zone I spotted the same guard with the gun from the evening before. He gave me a nod and a smile.

After the presentation there were more photographs. A bank of photographers were calling us to look this way and that. Then they wanted pictures of Bevan and me together — 'just the Kiwis' — but Sven was having a ball and he didn't want to step aside.

An official asked for my athletes' card (with your name and race number) to put on display at the Olympic museum in Lausanne, so I signed it and gave it to her. Then I saw Sarah [Ulmer], who'd jumped the barrier near the finish line. She was emotional and told me later that the meaning of her own gold sank in for her as she watched me win and be presented with my medal. Seeing her made me think of Roger, so Sarah called him for me on her phone. The three of us had been together since 1994. It had been some journey. All those years, trying to figure out if it was financially possible to be full-time athletes, the ups and downs, and here we were at the Olympics in Athens with gold medals around our necks. Roger's voice came on the line but he was too choked up to talk; there were just these guttural noises coming from the phone.

Roger Mortimer

Sarah won her gold medal in the early hours of 23 August. It was a Monday, 2 a.m., my birthday. Hamish's race was the following Thursday. Sarah had been expected to win. She was world champion, having won earlier that year in Melbourne where she broke the world record. Australian Katie Mactier and the Dutch girl, Leontine van Morsel, and Sarah herself had since all broken that record, but it would have been a shock if she hadn't won given the year she'd had. It was still very very exciting and meant everything to her. For her personally, she needed to close it out, and to go in as hot favourite and win was amazing.

Hamish's race was more emotional. Triathlon can be a bit of a horse race and there were a lot of guys who could have claimed it. When Sarah won, it might have been understandable for me to feel worried for Hamish: here they were, both chasing the same goal, and Sarah had achieved it. But, you know, I really wasn't. I knew what great shape he was in.

After Bevan won the worlds, the question couldn't have been more sharply defined: was Hamish Carter prepared to step aside? That was the perfect scenario for us leading into Athens. Bevan had made Hamish the underdog, the veteran who'd had a good career but was now expected to fade away. The thing is, nothing motivates Hamish more than proving people wrong about him.

I watched the triathlon at home with my partner, Megan, and our two-year-old son, Sebastian, who is Hamish's number-one fan. When they dropped Riederer, and then Hamish applied the pressure onto Bevan, I was up on my feet. Megan was worried about Sebastian because I was shouting at the television. I didn't dare to hope because there had been so many setbacks over the years, but when he got that two or three metres' break I thought, 'Oh my God, it's going to happen!'

I bawled my eyes out for about 10 minutes. I went out onto the street; it was pitch black. I had to get out of the house but I left the door open and my two-year-old came running after me. I was overwhelmed. I knew how hard it had been for Hamish and now here was a guy who was going to die a happy man.

It was immensely gratifying to see two people who are special to me fulfil their dreams. I could see parallels with the movie *Jerry Maguire*, about a manager and his client, a gridiron wide-receiver who isn't quite making it, but who finally becomes a superstar. The real story is about their relationship; how it's much more than agent and player, it's the shared journey of good friends. It sounds cheesy but that element of the movie was spot on. Hamish is one of my closest friends. That's why Athens was so emotional. Same with Sarah. My happiness for them was as their friend, and only very secondarily as their manager.

Of course, as their manager, you wouldn't even dream it. In Sydney, I'd imagined how incredible it would be to manage or be involved with a gold medallist but I never believed it would happen to me. I watched [pursuit winner] van Morsel doing her victory lap and when I saw Simon Whitfield receive his medal, I thought, 'We will never win that race'. Then it happens twice in four days. I'm still pinching myself.

I'm proud of their Olympic success for their sake, because they're the only people who made the sacrifice. Chris Pilone, myself and Brendon, Sarah's partner and coach, all played our parts, but they're the only ones who had the guts to do it. If they had got ninth or 10th, I still would have had a job, my life would have gone on. Same for Brendon and Sarah's father, Gary, and for Marisa. It would have been a blow for us, but life would go on. Gary's a pharmacist, Brendon's a sales rep. We wouldn't have spent every waking moment thinking about it. Sarah and Hamish would have.

Marisa

The party went very late at our place. The race was on at 7 p.m., prime time, and with the way it unfolded the television ratings were through the roof — way above the highest-rating All Black test match. It seemed as though the whole country had watched and it struck a chord with a lot of people. The number who called me — friends, family, but also clients I'd worked with — was amazing. The television people turned up again next morning and wanted to know how I was going to spend the first day of Hamish's reign as Olympic champion. Well, it was Friday, Austin's swimming day, so we were going to the pool. The cameras tagged along and filmed Austin in the pool. When he saw the television replays of the end of the race, all he wanted to know was why Daddy had fallen over. Then he announced that he was going to go to the Olympics. I asked what he was going to do there? Austin replied, 'I'm going to get Daddy.' That sums up his thoughts about it all.

Hamish rang again that morning and said that he was going to get on a plane and come straight home. I talked him out of it. It was only a couple of days until the closing ceremony and I firmly believed he should stay. The previous Olympics, when he was so down, he got hammered and so the closing was a bit of a blur. This time he could enjoy the experience and just be happy.

I'd gone off to doping control to give a urine sample and by the time I was done everyone was gone. All of a sudden it was over. I was thinking, 'Can I have the crowd back please? Can I celebrate some more?'

I was keen to get home and couldn't wait to share it with Marisa. The closing ceremony didn't seem that important. I didn't feel the need to go out and celebrate, I was just on such a high anyway. A lot of athletes who party after their events are trying to dull the pain of disappointment. I'd been away a long time, three months, and I felt like the job was done. Mission accomplished. I wanted to be back in Auckland with the people closest to me. But Marisa said, 'What's a few more days after three months?' And she was right. I'm glad I stayed.

I was so naïve. I had no idea what the win would mean. I didn't think it would make much difference to how people viewed me or thought of my career. It was a big race, yes, but it was just a race. I've done hundreds of races, won some and lost many. I thought people in New Zealand would be happy for me and there'd be a bit of a fuss for a few days, and then it would quieten down and life would more or less go back to normal. Boy, was I wrong.

Roger knew better. He warned Marisa to be prepared. I never anticipated the power that victory would have, that the interest in it would go on and on and never seem to fade. Maybe it was the image of two Kiwis dominating at an Olympics. For people who stop to talk to me in the street or who are in the audience when I give speeches, the impact of that image doesn't weaken.

In terms of personal satisfaction, Athens was everything. I would give up every race I've won for that single victory. That's how out of kilter the Olympics are. Everything rests on this one race that comes around only once in four years. You would have to win half a dozen world championships to match an Olympic gold medal. If you told people overseas that you'd won a world championship in triathlon, they wouldn't necessarily know what that meant. If you say you won an Olympic gold medal, it's a show-stopper. The Olympics is an international currency that everyone recognises. I was totally satisfied. It wouldn't have mattered to me if I'd never raced again.

AFTERGLOW

It's a strange experience to wake one morning and realise you are an Olympic champion. I didn't feel too flash. My hip was bloody sore from when I'd collapsed across the line. There must have been a rock under the blue carpet of the finishing chute where I landed. It felt like I'd broken the damn thing. I swung my legs off the bed and sat there, still half asleep, with my head in my hands. I had a big headache, though I don't know why. We'd had a pretty full-on night but I'd only drunk a couple of beers. The Greeks are big on white marble; it was everywhere in the Games village and the glare didn't help my head. As I squinted around the room, my gaze fell upon my room-mate and a 'visitor' — some girl he'd dragged home. 'Good for you,' I thought.

Then the table in the middle of the room came into focus. Among the clutter on top were a wreath and a medal. I was suddenly wide awake. Holy crap, it really happened! I'm the Olympic champion! Instantly, I was walking on air.

Just how demanding the course had been was brought home to me when I looked at the race results and saw how far behind some of the big names had finished. Tim Don (England), who would later beat me in the 2006 World Championships, was three-and-a-half minutes down. Robertson and Ivan Rana (Spain) were another minute back, while Gaag was five-and-a-half minutes behind. They'd all won world championships and had six titles between them, yet they'd been obliterated.

Not surprisingly, with Bevan and me finishing one-two, there was a real buzz among the Kiwis. A lot of people were full of stories about how confident they'd been about our chances and it turned out a couple of them had backed up their conviction with cash. One, apparently, won enough to pay for his trip to Europe. I'm not a gambler and would have hated to know that people were risking their money on me, but when I heard about the bets, I remembered seeing the name Centrebet. It had been on the dropdown menu bar on the computer at our training base in Pau — alongside sites with such dubious names as Monster Melons. Obviously someone had been checking the odds.

In the end I was glad that I stayed for the closing ceremony, which was such a complete contrast to my experience in Sydney, where I was drowning my sorrows. Even so, I couldn't wait to get home to enjoy it with Marisa and the kids, and get back to my ordinary life.

On the flight home, I sat next to Sir Murray Halberg. That was really cool. He's such a grounded person, very respected, and so good for the athletes to have around. I'd met him for the first time at the Commonwealth Games in 2002 where he'd also played a mentoring role with the team. He'd get together with groups of athletes and, although I hadn't talked to him personally, he's got such mana that something positive rubs off just from having him there. The Silver Ferns told me how he'd put things in perspective for them. Having lived a full and impressive life, he was able to look back over all that he'd experienced to see things for what they are. Without minimising the importance of the Olympics, he'd told the netball girls that his real gold medals were his children. He'd talked about how short the sporting life is and told them to enjoy it, for goodness' sake, and not get consumed by your desire to win, because in 20 years' time it won't be the be-all and end-all of your life.

Dave Currie decided that the whole team should travel home together in economy class. I thought it was a top idea. I'd back whatever Dave said because he was so good to us in Athens and at the Manchester Commonwealth Games. So we were all in economy from London to Los Angeles, but on the LA to Auckland leg, I was put in business class, although I didn't realise it until I stepped on the plane. I sat down in my seat and thought, 'This is comfortable' — but my conscience got the better of me. I went back in the plane and told Murray some bullshit story about the seats being mixed up. He didn't want special treatment and I knew he wouldn't accept it if he thought that I was just giving it to him. Soon after, a flight attendant approached me and said that another business class seat was available. Well, you don't look a gift horse in the mouth twice! So I ended up sitting right next to Sir Murray Halberg. We didn't talk a lot because we were both so tired, but he asked about my race and I told him it was one of those rare days when everything clicked, how I'd felt strong the whole way. I asked whether he'd ever experienced that.

'Yes, two or three times,' he said, and asked how often it had happened for me.

'A couple of times,' I told him.

'Oh,' Murray said, 'you've probably got one more to go then, one more race like that left in you. It only happens two or three times in a person's career.'

I think he nodded off after that, or maybe I did, but it was a special moment for me. He's very matter of fact, but what he says is quite profound. He's a humble guy and you can see that in his book, *A Clean Pair of Heels*. It was published in 1963, three years after he won the Olympic 5000 metres in Rome. The chapter about becoming an Olympic champion is called 'A Mere Mortal'. I think that's typical of the man, and there's one passage in particular that holds meaning for me now. 'I had always imagined an Olympic champion was something more than a mere mortal; in fact, a god. Now I knew he was just a human being.'

I hadn't read his book back then, otherwise we would have had a lot more to talk about on that flight. I hadn't realised how similar our

Olympic experiences had been. He'd found himself at absolute rock bottom after failing in Melbourne in 1956. He finished 11th of the 12 finalists in the 1500 metres and the result sent him into a black despair. It had seemed almost like a death to him, because his whole life had been aimed at succeeding there. That's exactly how it felt for me in Sydney. And his gold medal in Rome was like mine in Athens.

It might sound cocky of me to compare myself with him but I was stunned by how much I could relate to — right down to how he collapsed to the ground as he reached the tape in Rome, landing in a heap. In the first chapter of his book, he talks about being overawed by his first Olympics, of running in a blur with no real plan or confidence. As his race unravelled, he talks of a 'heart-stopping, mind-blanking terror' of the kind he'd felt years earlier when ripped off his feet by a vicious undertow on a West Coast beach. That sense of helplessness is what I felt when the race slipped away from me in Sydney.

'I stood alone in the middle of it all, dejected, bitter, borne down by a sense of failure,' he writes. 'I wasn't upset so much by the feeling that I had failed. I knew it was in me to do a lot better but I had promised my coach, Arthur Lydiard, I would bring back a medal, and I had failed miserably. A lot of people back in New Zealand had expected me to do well and I felt like I had let them down. For the moment I seemed to have lost my way.'

His life had been all about those Olympics, just as mine had been about following this damned dream, this belief that somehow I was destined to win the Olympic triathlon and that it would happen in Sydney. 'The defeat I suffered seemed to have made a mockery of the whole effort,' Halberg wrote. Well, ditto to that.

After returning home, Halberg went on a long, solo hiking trip in the South Island wilderness hoping to clear his head and make up his mind about whether to continue in the sport. He came to the realisation that one disappointing race didn't make him a poor athlete. This is how that chapter of his book finishes: 'Finally I did convince myself. I had, after all, already succeeded in getting as far as an Olympic final. It was in me to do better. Yes, I was going to have another try. And this time, nothing would stop me from succeeding.'

Reading about Halberg got me thinking again about the nature of success, of victory. I don't think it's about winning a particular race, so much as not letting the failures destroy you. It's about turning the failures around, learning the lessons those disappointments can teach you. Everyone remembers the moment of arriving at some milestone, or the moment of some important achievement. What's less readily recalled is how you fought through the rough patches. To me, that is the true victory; it's in the overcoming.

I have no doubt that if I hadn't gone through such misery at the Sydney Olympics and had to face the self-doubt that flowed from that, they wouldn't have hung a gold medal around my neck in Athens on 26 August 2004. Even if I hadn't won, I'd still feel that the experience had helped me grow, both as an athlete and as a person. I was proud to be in Athens and to have done well enough to earn the chance to create a better Olympic memory.

I assume Halberg's 5000 metres in Rome in 1960 was one of those rare days we'd talked about on the plane. 'Audacious' is the only word I can think of to describe his tactics when he sprinted with three laps to go — something that was unheard of at the time. He and Lydiard had decided that they would catch his rivals by surprise, get a gap and bank on Halberg's stamina. He wrote how, on the final lap, his body was screaming for him to stop, but he thought of everything he'd put into getting to that moment. 'It was my destiny to win, not to quit,' he wrote. In the last kilometre of my own race, when it was down to Bevan and me, gold or silver, there was no way I was going to accept second.

Halberg has been such a special champion and, in the weeks after Athens, I came to realise that I wanted to be not only an Olympic champion, but a worthy one. I didn't want to just fade away. I wanted to continue to race well, for myself but also to honour the title and people such as Halberg and my hero, John Walker. I would have loved to have crossed the line wearing the iconic black singlet, as they had. It would have made it that extra bit special, but on such a hot day, in such a long race, it's not the best colour to race in. I remember how moving it had been for me as a primary school kid to watch Walker win at the 1976 Montreal Olympics. I couldn't believe that I'd also had the chance to experience that. Athens gave me the wreath and the medal, but it has also given me a deep sense of contentment, the kind that comes from having achieved your ultimate goal.

Walking through the arrival gates at Auckland International Airport, I was struck by how big Austin had grown. Phoebe, too; she was three months old when I left, so I'd been away half her life. That's one of the main reasons I found it hard being away for long periods after having kids. The cost of those times apart was brought home to me a couple of evenings later when Marisa had a night out with the girls. Phoebe got really upset and wouldn't stop crying. I tried everything — bottle, wind — but she was still screaming. Austin looked up at me with his big eyes and said, 'Daddy, Phoebe doesn't know who you are.' Talk about out of the mouths of babes. Intuitively, he'd known exactly what the problem was. She hadn't seen me or heard my voice for so long that she must have been wondering who the hell this stranger was.

My absences were hard on Austin, too. Marisa talked about how reluctant he'd been when she tried to show him replays of the race as a way of explaining where Daddy was. It took another couple of years to figure out why. After I came home from the 2006 World Championships, I told Austin that I'd really missed him. He said he'd seen me on television and wanted to know why I hadn't said 'hello' to him. That's when the penny dropped.

It was good to get back to normality, reconnecting with friends, talking about anything but triathlon. Jason Windhager is one of those friends. We've known each other since we rowed together at Auckland Grammar. He's a businessman now and it's so good spending time with him and his wife, Kate, because our friendship doesn't revolve around sport. It's nice to have that balance. That's not to say they aren't right behind me. Jason watched the race on television until it got too much for him and he jumped in his car and went for a drive. He knows what I put into it, what it meant to me, and he wanted it to turn out right. When I spoke to him afterwards, he said, 'Well, you can die happy now.'

Everyone seemed thrilled by my win. Strangers would stop me to say that they'd watched it on television. An elderly lady in Queen Street told me about the impact it had on her and her eyes were brimming with tears. Seeing the pleasure it brought others was an undeniable buzz. It seemed as though half of New Zealand had watched the race. To this day, I'm still surprised by how it captured the imagination of people from all walks of life. I heard so many stories: an old schoolmate who'd heard the result while piloting a KLM passenger jet, another who watched in a pub in Ireland, someone else who saw it in South Africa. It reached out to Kiwis everywhere.

After I got back to Auckland, we had a Carter family dinner and toasted the win. Though it's the family way not to go overboard when one of us does well, I knew how pleased they were for me and the kick they got out of it.

Clive Carter

Because Sydney was so dreadful, when the Athens Olympics came around, the family decided that we couldn't go through that again. 'You go away and do your best,' we told Hamish. 'We'll be right with you emotionally, but we're not coming.'

Pat and I were in Wanaka with some of Hamish's aunts and uncles. The television wasn't working where we were staying, so I went to Edgewater Resort on the day of the triathlon and explained the situation to the manager. He was marvellous and arranged for us to watch it in one of the bars. We went over that evening with trepidation, fearing another disaster. As the race progressed, word must have got around that Hamish was doing well because people started to pour out of the dining room, and there ended up being a huge crowd. There was a real sense of community; all these strangers were as excited as we were.

One guy said to me, 'Your boy is going to win this.'

'How do you work that out?' I asked.

'Just look at the determination in his eyes!'

By the end, the whole hotel was screaming and yelling. Total strangers were congratulating us; the hotel brought out bottles of champagne and a cake with 'Congratulations on your boy' written on top. We stayed until the early hours of the next morning. It was an unforgettable night. We'd dared not hope.

26 August 2004, Athens Olympic Triathlon, TV One	
Time	*Viewers*
7.00 p.m. Triathlon begins	783,000
8.00 p.m. Nearing the end of the bike leg	932,000
8.30 p.m. Midway through the run	1,044,000
8.45 p.m. Nearing the finish	1,156,000
Highest-rating test match of 2004: All Blacks v Australia	678,000

Barry Cleal

I watched the race, of course, and followed what he had to say about it afterwards in the media. If there were things I didn't know about Hamish, I discovered them after Athens. He didn't let anyone who had ever helped him off the hook. I've probably only seen him once or twice since those school rowing days when I coached him, and when they don't forget you, well to be honest I was bursting with pride. To think that we'd dropped so far out of touch and he'd reached such a level of success, yet he still had time to say, 'Hey, I appreciate what that guy did.' When you're an old crusty, that's very special.

Marisa

Life became very hectic when Hamish got back, with a lot of media and corporate interest. It was interesting to compare it with how things had been after Sydney. In different ways, it was hard after both his failure and his success. No one wanted to ask Hamish about Sydney, so they'd often ask me. Then, after Athens, it was, 'Oh, how's Hamish?' And that is fine; I'm really proud of him. But after having children it gets a little tougher because you lose so much of your sense of self anyway, because you're a mother and not working as much. That was challenging for both of us. I remember saying in a radio interview after he won in Athens that I couldn't wait for him to get back home so that he could change some nappies.

I was looking forward to a rest, spending time with friends, maybe playing some golf. That shows how naïve I was. I thought that there might be a bit of a fuss for a week or two and then life would drift back to normal. I soon discovered that Roger's phone had been ringing from the moment I crossed the line in Athens.

The first thing I did when I got home was have some toast, because Europe doesn't understand toast. Then I wanted good coffee (you can't find it in Greece), so we went down the road to a café. It was like I'd been dropped into an alien world. Here was I, brown as a berry and skinny as a concentration camp survivor (I'd got a stomach bug after the race), surrounded by all these white people wearing jumpers and jackets. It was cold and grey, and a bit of a reality check, after the Olympics, where the athletes had been treated almost like gods when they ventured out of the village. Maybe that's what it's like for a junkie coming down or a one-hit rock star. But normality is exactly what I miss when I'm away. I was looking forward to relaxing with the family and recovering from the flight. So the last thing I wanted to do was to go out on my first night home.

I couldn't work out why, but Rog was pushing me to make a guest appearance on the TV show *Sports Café*, which was filmed live, and I eventually relented. It's a lot of fun, and I soon blew off my fatigue when Marc Ellis drove this truck into the studio and almost into the front row of the audience. Then Ric Salizzo, the presenter, tossed me the keys and said, 'It's yours!' Hyundai gave one to Marisa as well. I was stoked. I hadn't had a car sponsor since losing Subaru after Sydney. Roger did a great job working out which companies I was suited to, and Hyundai and Sanitarium had both signed on, but Roger had been talking to them well before I won that race. After that gold medal, there was a lot of interest and it might have been tempting to take as much money as possible. However, you soon realise that a relationship with good people in a good company is more important. We didn't do any short-term stuff; most of my sponsor partnerships have lasted five years or more.

Roger Mortimer

Hamish and Sarah both told me when they got back from Athens that they wanted to stick with the people who had stuck with them. They could have said, 'Show me the money', but instead they said, 'Promise me nothing is going to change'. It was like being part of a team and we could all celebrate together. One of the most incredible

> nights I've had was a combined sponsors' night that Sarah and Hamish put on after they got home. Nowhere in the world would you have two good friends celebrating Olympic gold medals with the same group: McDonald's, Nike, Vodafone, Avanti, Purina, Sanitarium, Hyundai, Hewlett Packard, Air New Zealand and Cyco.

I was suddenly in demand on the speaking circuit. The idea of a couple of hundred people paying good money to listen to me was daunting at first. I may even have suggested to Roger that we didn't charge in case I bored everyone, but I enjoyed it almost straight away, and the audience seemed to as well. I don't get stage fright. Maybe I take after Dad, who is the family speechmaker. Whenever there's an occasion, Dad will stand up and make a little speech. He's always pretty eloquent. It's all in the telling. Rather than getting nervous and choking up, I'd remind myself that I'm just talking about what I do. Sharing your experiences with people who take joy from it is quite empowering — an ego trip really. You can say the dumbest thing and often they'll laugh. You can see how some people find it addictive, and I guess that's why at occasions such as weddings there's always someone who doesn't want to give up the microphone.

The New Zealand public responded to my win in a way that I never imagined, which was amazing and humbling. A couple of pieces from that time stand out in my scrapbook. The *New Zealand Herald* chose me as winner of its Sportsmanship Award for the year. 'Sportsmanship can take many forms,' the paper's chief sports writer, David Leggat, wrote. 'It could be a helping hand offered to a fallen rival; an admission that a catch had not been fairly held . . . the acknowledgment that your golf ball moved a millimetre, though only you had witnessed it. Or it could be picking yourself up out of the ashes of a broken dream, reapplying mind and body and turning despair into triumph, all achieved without an ugly word or deed along the way. So it is that the *Herald*'s Sportsmanship Award for the year goes to Olympic triathlon champion Hamish Carter.'

And Tony Smith, writing an end-of-year piece in *The Press*, described the Athens triathlon as 'the race that stopped a nation'. 'Those titanic twins, Caroline and Georgina Evers-Swindell, set the trend with their double sculls victory at Lake Schinias. Cyclist supreme Sarah Ulmer smashed the world record three times on her inexorable ride to pursuit glory. But the Kiwi quinella in the triathlon had to be the highlight for me — and maybe a million or so Kiwis glued to their television sets.

'Those of us beachside in Athens were blessed with a bird's-eye view as a screaming, leaping Hamish Carter collapsed across the finish line — so close he could have kicked sand into my laptop. We barely had time to blink in the brilliant sunlight as Carter was followed home by Kiwi compatriot Bevan Docherty . . . After the failure of our equestrian team and the becalming of our boaties, Docherty or Carter were our last great white hopes of a third Olympic gold. All eyes — even Australian peepers — were on Docherty. The Taupo triathlete was the world champion. He had usurped Carter, for so long New Zealand's undisputed No. 1. Make no mistake — triathlon isn't a team sport. Docherty was out there under that impossibly blue sky in that relentless 35 degree heat to win the gold medal for himself. "Everything seems to be coming together this year . . . I feel like I'm starting to reach my peak," he had told me a month out from the Olympics.

'I will never forget Docherty's dignity after the race as he came to terms with the fact that 2004 had, for him, a silver lining instead of a golden hue. "It's a pity I didn't come away with the gold, but who better to lose it to than Hamish, my team-mate." Who better indeed? No disrespect to Docherty, but I am glad that Carter crossed the line first at Vouliagmeni. I had seen the affable Aucklander suffer the most devastating defeat of his career at Sydney in 2000 . . . Few New Zealanders appreciate the sport's international depth. Any one of 10 — maybe 20 — athletes could win the Olympic gold on any given day. But on August 26, 2004, the day belonged to Carter, a curly-topped beanpole of a bloke from New Zealand. Minutes before two New Zealand flags fluttered from the Vouliagmeni flagpole, an ecstatic Carter confided to the Kiwi media corps: "I just can't believe it, man . . . I'm stoked." So were we, Hamish. A whole nation was thrilled that after the setback in Sydney this proud Kiwi battler chose to tri, tri, tri and tri again.'

COACHING AN OLYMPIC CHAMPION

Coaches are your link to the real world. Often, as an athlete, you are buried in your own programme or so tired that you can't see the big picture. It's the coach's job to harness your ability, hone and develop it, and deliver you to the big race in the best possible shape. They need to be a friend, motivator, strategic planner, psychologist, mentor and, sometimes, a plain old stubborn bugger who won't budge from the plan. The best instinctively know which hat to wear at what time and I've been fortunate to work with some of the best.

Chris Pilone was my main coach from 2001 through to my retirement in 2006. Under his direction I won bronze at the Commonwealth Games, silver at the world championships and gold at the Olympic Games.

Chris Pilone

Like most New Zealanders, I watched Hamish Carter's disappointing performance at the 2000 Sydney Olympics. He was 29 and I assumed he might compete for another year or so and then drift out of the sport. So I was somewhat surprised when he rang me in 2001 proposing a formal coaching association.

Hamish was a member of the Bays Cougars club, where I was a distance-running coach, and after some discussion I became his overall coach. Mark Bone remained as his swimming coach. Most of my coaching background came through my own running career and also from Athletics New Zealand's coach education programme. I'd become a keen road cyclist and had a good knowledge of road cycling training, occasionally calling on the knowledge of Auckland cycling coach Paul Leitch.

At first, Hamish used a system of alternating weeks, where he emphasised cycling one week and running the next, with four days of swimming every week. Using this regime he won bronze at the 2002 Commonwealth Games. Early in 2003, he proposed a dramatic change in his training whereby he completely rebuilt the structure of the standard week. Every day he would train very hard and completely overload his system. He would back this up for 3–5 days then take 1–2 days to recover. It wasn't always pretty and there was a lot of time he overcooked it, but eventually, together, we made it work.

This was typical of Hamish; he was always looking for ways to improve how we did things. My initial reaction was that it was a stupid idea, but we decided to give it a try, and it turned out to be a very good system for him, resulting in a significant increase in mileage.

Often he'd head off to Pauanui or Rotorua for mini training camps to provide some variety. A standard Pauanui camp might involve a 160 km ride from Auckland, a two-hour run the next day, a swim, bike and a run the third day and another long ride on the fourth. This produced good results immediately. Despite having done no speed work for running or cycling, he won the 2003 Aussie Sprint champs (750 m/20 km/5 km) over a distance that doesn't suit him. He was set back by a bout of influenza during winter but performed relatively well at that year's world championships in Queenstown, placing fifth and qualifying for the 2004 Athens Olympics.

Even so, I wasn't totally confident with his two-month sharpening period that led up to the 2003 Worlds. It became apparent that he was well suited to good, high-quality aerobic work for both running and cycling, but he had to be very careful with anything that pushed him even slightly harder.

Carter turned 33 during Olympic year and as a runner was relatively slow. His only chance of out-finishing his rivals at the end of a 10 km running leg of an Olympic-distance triathlon was to get to the final kilometre with more left in the tank than his opposition. For 2004, I planned a greater strength-based programme, with his running and cycling tempo work mainly being at lactate threshold intensity (the level of effort where the body begins to produce lactic acid in the muscles, thereby causing muscle performance to diminish rapidly). The small amount of VO2 max work (maximum oxygen intake) would be carefully placed and controlled.

For Olympic year we did a single periodisation (one build-up of training aimed ultimately at one target race) and didn't try to peak for the 2004 Worlds in May. I also coach Nathan Richmond, the third member of the Olympic Games triathlon team, and was appointed assistant to the team's manager and coach, Mark Elliott. This enabled me to have direct input into all of our Olympic arrangements and pre-Olympic training camp in Pau, southern France. I've always had a good relationship with Mark, who was an outstanding high-performance manager for Triathlon New Zealand. Mark challenged me as a coach and was quite blunt about asking me what I planned to do to put Hamish Carter on the podium in Athens. Although we were coaching athletes who were arch-rivals, this never affected our relationship.

Hamish had a trouble-free Olympics build-up in New Zealand. He did a big aerobic base, from January to June, and that provided an ideal platform. During his five weeks in camp in France, he trained better than ever before. We had a great environment with development athletes there as well and, for some of the time, Olympic marathon runner Dale Warrander, who I also coached. The athletes trained very hard but had a lot of fun, too. The training and low-key environment was a significant factor in the success Docherty and Carter enjoyed in Athens.

The only slight negative in France was that Hamish was so fit he started dishing out severe beatings in training to various training hacks and, on occasion, to Nathan Richmond, which I believe affected Richmond's own performance at the Olympics.

Liam Scopes, who was a regular training hack for Hamish at Pau, was very good at making Hamish moderate his training. Hamish was so fit that he kept wanting to go harder and longer in training. Between us, Liam and I managed to keep him under relative control.

Exactly two weeks out from the Olympics, Hamish did a hard bike-to-run session — a hard two-hour ride followed by eight 1000-metre runs on the track with a 45-second jog recovery. Liam Scopes, Clark Ellice and Kris Gemmell acted as his hacks, taking turns to pace him. The session went very well, despite being in the middle of the afternoon and very hot. After that I thought he was a likely winner in Athens, but intentionally kept my view from him.

For the last two weeks before the race, he did easier training with one run session of 200 m in 33–34 seconds, followed by 200 m floating along in 40 seconds. He did this for five laps, jogged for five minutes, and then repeated the session. Liam Scopes did part of the session to make sure that Hamish didn't go harder than required, because he doesn't respond well to a lot of fast work. It tends to cause his form to tail off, rather than bring him on.

Race day was quite simply unforgettable. The victories in consecutive races of Snell and Murray Halberg at the 1960 Olympics remain for me New Zealand's finest sporting hour, but it was nice to play a small part in something that perhaps can be mentioned in the same breath.

In 2006, Hamish was second at his 15th and last world championships. He has been in the top six on eight occasions and won a dozen World Cup races, more than anyone else. I put his success, longevity and consistency down to two factors: good health and his ability to pace his training. He has a very good immune system and seldom gets sick, and he's been largely free of injury. Once he gets rolling on his training programme, he gets fitter and fitter and fitter.

I don't rate either Carter or Docherty as New Zealand's most talented triathletes. I'd say that would be Richmond and Kris Gemmell. But Carter and Docherty can absorb big amounts of training and hold together.

Carter can instinctively judge pace and effort without needing to wear a heart-rate monitor. I can ask him to do a 20-minute run at lactate threshold and he'll slot into that pace intuitively. As a result, he's able to do his training at the desired intensity. Mental toughness on race day can also be a factor, but it's irrelevant if you're not in the right physical condition. It's also a variable. If you looked at how Hamish raced in Athens or at the 2006 Worlds, you'd think he was bulletproof, but I've seen the other side. He's had his share of highs and lows.

I'm not a great believer in sports psychology. At the highest level, the training programme is everything. It has to be the right training and it has to be the right timing. We got both right for Athens, as you can see by the beautiful running rhythm Carter maintained all the way to the tape.

A year out from an Olympics or the world champs, there are 30 to 40 people who can win. Some don't get selected. Some get sick or injured. Some don't time their training right and some do inappropriate training. A week out from the race there may be six contenders. Then some don't handle the pressure. If you survive that process of elimination, you're right in the hunt. Get those basics right and sometimes you can achieve an unbelievable result.

Mark Bone became my swimming coach when I was recovering from breaking my collarbone on Alpe d'Huez in 1994 and was still responsible for keeping my swimming up to the mark when I retired. He was there for me through all the highs and lows.

Mark Bone

Triathletes, as a breed, are a bit more out there, a bit brasher, a bit more passionate about their sport. It's quite humbling for them to come into an environment where the swimmers aren't that interested in who they are.

Hamish, though, got on well with the elite swimmers. Once a week the squad would play golf and it seemed to be a competition to see who could take the most piss out of the others. Sometimes we'd be doubled up with laughter. It was hugely beneficial because it provided an outlet and a break from the grind.

Swimming does three things. One, it improves your swimming. Two, it increases your cardiovascular fitness and helps your running and cycling more than cycling and running can alone. Because your body is in a prone position during swimming you use your heart and lungs and all of your muscles, whereas biking and running isolates your legs. Three, swimming helps recovery from hard bikes and runs.

One of Hamish's strengths is his ability to read his own body. He can differentiate between when his body is tired and in need of recovery and when it's just tired from the training. Sometimes when an athlete is tired, overloading with more training may be exactly what's needed.

He's very consistent in the way he prepares and that's reflected in how he races. But he's also always looking for new ideas and is willing to challenge his coaches. Sometimes you have to sell the concept to Hamish; explain it in detail, allow him to absorb it and wait for it to come back to you in his own way. It's like sowing a seed. He and I have never had a disagreement, but we've certainly had lots of discussions.

One of Hamish's great strengths is his wife. Marisa is one tough cookie. She's a former great swimmer and swimming has given her a toughness that she applies to her life. Hamish is his own man, but she is one person who can bring him down to earth. She puts his feet on the ground when he needs it.

Prior to Athens, Hamish wasn't swimming well but that's not unusual when a triathlete is running superbly. The leanness in the upper body, while good for running, isn't ideal for swimming. I regret that I couldn't go over to work with him. It was an incredibly stressful and exhausting time for my wife, Sue, and me because we had borrowed heavily to build a new pool as a base for our business and were flat out getting it ready for opening day. Even so, I came very close to getting on a plane to Pau. His swimming was a risk, but I knew from Chris that he was incredibly fit.

I don't usually get nervous watching races, but I admit I was when he was so far back after the swim. That changed when I saw how he climbed the hill. I was confident the whole way through the run. I said to Sue, 'This bugger's going to win.' I was coaching Bevan too, but

I was thrilled for Hamish because I was there when he went through the horrible lows of Sydney.

Jack Ralston, was my main coach from 1984, when I was a schoolboy, until 2001. Together we climbed to the top of the world rankings, won a World Cup series, and silver and bronze at world championships. Jack shared those highs with me as well as the low of the Sydney Olympics.

Jack Ralston

Part of the reason Hamish survived at the top for so long was that we didn't flog anaerobic work, we didn't kill him with too much speed work and we didn't over-race. His programme would have no more than two or three peaks in a year. We picked our races, which meant that he never went into one unfit, although he may have lacked a bit of speed because we were putting that in later in the season.

The basis of my training methods came from Arthur Lydiard, melded with other influences, such as some techniques Arch Jelley used with John Walker and the more scientific approach of the Europeans to training different threshold levels. Lydiard had pretty much done that by sticking his finger in the air. When I read the scientific research, I realised that what Lydiard was doing actually had a scientific basis.

Lydiard was misinterpreted; he wasn't the long, slow, distance guy. I trained with him and his athletes in the mid-1960s when I was a teenager and they'd honk along at 56-minute 10-mile pace, but doing it comfortably.

The goal is to get the athlete's body used to running 10,000 m at as high a heart rate as can be managed, but just under the threshold where your body is producing lactic acid. You push up the ceiling of how much lactate your body can handle.

That's what I tried to do with Hamish — convince him that he could push even harder into that zone. He was hard-nosed enough to do that, to throw the bloody heart-rate monitor away. He never raced wearing one.

The decision not to go to the opening ceremony of the Athens Olympics was crucial, as was Chris getting into his ear that the damage was going to be done on the bike. In my heart I believed that he was going to win. Everything seemed spot on. I had an inner calm about it, so much so that I booked for my wife, Margaret, and I to go to the stage show *Evita*. I recorded the race and watched it when we got home. Prior to watching it, however, I made the mistake of looking at my cellphone and there were something like 28 messages on it. I said to Margaret: 'Something's happened.' We sat in bed watching until 1 a.m. I had tears running down my face.

BEING SOMEBODY

I'd hardly settled into home life, before I was off again. This time I was bound for Chicago. Roger and Sarah and I were off to the McDonald's world headquarters for a meet-and-greet with some of the senior executives there.

When we first linked up with McDonald's some people questioned the association of fast food with health and fitness. We thought hard about it, but in the end I didn't have a problem with it. Rog and I had the opportunity to see where the company was heading, taking a leadership role in the industry by giving customers a choice and educating them about what they were eating. I've always eaten McDonald's, along with my kids. I enjoy it, but no one is saying that you should eat it every day. It's that old rowing lesson about balance again. If you have a balanced diet and an active lifestyle, there's nothing wrong with treating yourself from time to time. I think that together we made a positive impact.

It was a shock to be back on a plane so soon, but it was a good chance to get some space to reflect. The Olympics is such a world apart, that what that means to your life takes a while to sink in.

After Sarah won the pursuit, she still had the points race to come, so she couldn't afford to dwell on it too much or let loose and really celebrate. It was only after she'd finished her events and was watching my race that it hit her.

Sarah Ulmer

My partner, Brendon, and I saw Hamish get the gap on Bevan and the Swiss guy. It was great to be there, live, with the pressure off me, seeing Olympic gold being won by a mate. Watching Carter get his medal — that's when it hit home for me. I was bawling, and I hadn't even cried when I won.

It was only later that I found out that he'd had a small breakdown, like I had before my race. It's the nature of the gig. You're shoved into a compound with all these other people who are stressed about trying to achieve the same thing as you. It's like a pressure cooker: team meetings, medal tallies, people performing, people not performing, all the emails coming from home. The winch gets tighter and tighter and tighter. The night before my qualifying ride in the pursuit, Brendon and I were going over the schedule I'd need to ride to achieve my goal of recording the fastest time. It was a world record time. I looked at it and thought, 'Oh God, this is ridiculous'. I had tears running down my face, and Brendon just cracked up laughing at me. I had a bawl for a minute or two and then it was sweet. It's like the pressure valve gets opened.

Americans aren't shy about parading achievements. When Sarah and I gave our little speeches to the McDonald's executives, the event planners insisted that we wear our medals. We were obliged to wear them later, too, at a poster-signing session in one of their stores. We thought that no one would turn up to see a couple of foreigners they'd never heard of, but the queue went out the door and up the road. All because of an Olympic gold medal.

A less pleasant aspect of the trip was how Roger was treated. He was sidelined; barged aside by people wanting to speak to us. There were people telling us that we should be signing this or that big-money deal while our manager had been elbowed out of the room as if he were unworthy of being there. We were so busy it didn't register at the time, and it was a testament to Roger's humility that he took those hits and continued to do such a good job because it was worse than rude, it was unfair. People didn't understand how important he was to our success. Since Athens, he'd worked around the clock for both of us, which was tough on his wife and child. Sarah and I shouted him, Megan and Sebastian a holiday at Millbrook in Queenstown to say thank you, and at the Halberg Awards I got the chance to acknowledge him publicly (Sarah won the Halberg and Sportswoman of the Year Awards, while I won Sportsman of the Year). Sarah and I had paid for a table at the function so that we could invite some of the people who'd been so important in our careers. It was a cool night, especially as I finally got to meet my hero, John Walker, who presented me with my award. That was perfect; there's no one in the world I would rather have received it from. In my speech I thanked my supporters and made special mention of Roger. 'Rog,' I said, 'if there was ever a manager of the year, it's you.'

It would have been very easy to get caught up in it all, the speeches, school appearances, VIP invites. It was a buzz to see the looks on some of the school kids' faces; and strange but gratifying to think I might have the same impact on a few of them that Walker had on me when I was their age. I was so enthused by the reaction to my first school visit after winning in Athens that I spoke to Sarah about it.

Sarah Ulmer

He was fizzing and said the effect on the kids was incredible. About a week later, I had the same experience at Clevedon School in Auckland. A couple of parents stood up and spoke about how their kids used to only play computer games but were now off on their bikes four times a week. It sounds so cheesy, but one of the coolest things is the effect you can have on some people. People in hospital told me that watching my race was a turning point, motivating them to walk again, turn the page or turn their life around. Here was I, tied up in the often selfish world of athletics, and to think that something I'd done had had such a profound influence was pretty cool.

There's definitely a risk of your ego running riot. I was lucky to be able to come home from speaking engagements to my kids. I was just Dad to them. And Marisa made sure that there was time set aside for us as a family, otherwise that aspect of your life can end up playing third fiddle behind business and training. Roger isn't one to play the A-list game, and he didn't pass a lot of invitations on to me. I enjoy meeting people whose faces are familiar from being in the media, but I realise it's just hype; it's not a real life. Having had a little public recognition before Athens helped me keep it all in perspective. I think that's why it had more of an impact on Bevan and it took him a long time to return to top form.

Roger Mortimer

I don't think that Hamish, as a person, was ready to take on the mantle of Olympic champion in 2000, and I wasn't capable of managing one. But he's been a great champion since Athens. I haven't seen one iota of arrogance in Hamish Carter since that race. Had he won in Sydney, I think it would have been gushing from him. His personal development isn't just down to dealing with the failure of Sydney; becoming a father was also hugely grounding.

After two months of business commitments and appearances, but no training, it was time to flick the switch back to being an athlete. Roger set a date with Pilone and off I went. That concentrated the mind, because I didn't want to step out as the Olympic champion and race like a chump. After getting dropped while wearing the yellow jersey in the Tour de France one year, Lance Armstrong said that he hadn't done the jersey justice that day. My goal was to live up to the status that comes with the title. Roger and I blocked out periods when I wouldn't be available to sponsors — typically, three months during summer, when I was putting in a big mileage base, and a similar period in winter, when I was competing overseas. We gave plenty of notice so that they could plan accordingly and in the autumn of 2005 I flew out with the family to do some quality training in Victoria, Canada.

Simon Whitfield made all the arrangements: a house to rent,

babysitting, everything. He made it easy for me to get back to the basics of being an athlete, despite being one of my chief rivals. He was the defending Olympic champion when I won in Athens and yet went out of his way to help me. That says a lot about the guy, his generosity and confidence. We ended up running side by side at the world championships a few months later in September. We both know that he's the better runner but, whether the bike or the heat stung him that day, it was me who moved ahead. The conditions didn't suit me (a flat course, a hot day) and I finished fourth, but although I missed the medals, it was up there among my best performances.

Two weeks earlier I'd won the Chicago triathlon, shutting out American Hunter Kemper, a renowned runner who was world number one at the time, and Bevan. It was very satisfying to have Bevan and me dominate one of the biggest races in the United States. Following Athens, we were the guys everyone wanted to beat, and nowhere more so than in America. However at the worlds, I was the only Kiwi to fire. Sam Warriner, 16th, did best of the New Zealand women and I was followed, among the Kiwis, by Shane Reed, 11th, Terrenzo Bozzone, 27th, and Kris Gemmell, 38th. Neither Bevan nor Nathan Richmond, my team-mates in Athens, finished.

Great champions are those who win the big event but don't fade into obscurity afterwards. At times it was a real struggle, but I'd have been gutted if my form had tailed off after Athens. It's a bit brutal, but I take real pleasure from the fact that the two other Athens medallists (Bevan and Sven Riederer) haven't pulled a result at the world championships since. If Bevan reads this, I hope he gets pissed off and nails the next world champs.

Roger Mortimer

I've managed many athletes during my 13 years in the business and arguably the most naturally competitive was former All Black Zinzan Brooke. On a television quiz show one time there was a debate about the number of squares on a chessboard and Zinny challenged anyone who disagreed with him to take a bet on it. Hamish Carter would match Zinzan; he's very competitive about a lot of things.

I've never denied the rivalry that existed between Bevan and me. We both wanted to be the best in the world, but there was an extra dimension because we were vying to be the top New Zealander. I'm grateful he came along, even though he caused me grief when he won the 2004 World Championships and shunted me aside as top Kiwi. But it's unlikely that I would have won Athens without the spur he provided. Beating him remained important to me until I retired. That may sound a bit off, but it's actually a big compliment. If Bevan wasn't such a brilliant athlete, I wouldn't give him a second thought. The fact is, that on his day, there is no one tougher.

Bevan put in his best performance since Athens at the 2006 Melbourne Commonwealth Games in March, finishing second behind Aussie Brad Kahlefaeldt. Pilone and I had planned my season around the world championships in September and I couldn't be in top shape for both. It wasn't a hard choice. Although the Commonwealth Games has history and profile in New Zealand, it no longer has much prestige internationally. The Games attract about six of the world's top triathletes, after which the quality quickly drops. This was possibly my last year and I wanted to go out racing against the best, and the best field is at the world championships. I never doubted the logic of my decision but it wasn't easy knowing that I was nowhere near my best shape, especially when I was given the honour of being the New Zealand team's flagbearer. At the ceremony to announce who was flagbearer, I was called on to make a little speech to the athletes. I was a bit stuck as to what to say, knowing in my heart that it was highly unlikely I'd be in the medals. I reminded them they had the honour of representing New Zealand and that, no matter what, they must never give up. That came back to bite me during the run, when I was trying in vain to extract a kick of speed from my legs. Pilone yelled out, 'Don't forget what you said in that bloody speech!' I felt like telling him to shut up, but he was right. I grovelled as hard as I could and finished sixth, not too bad in the circumstances.

The women finished second (Sam Warriner), third (Andrea Hewitt) and fourth (Debbie Tanner), adding to the men's result of second (Bevan), fifth (Kris Gemmell) and me in sixth. I was pleased that the team had done well but at the same time a little peeved that Bevan had given me a pasting. Yet I knew I was right to stick with my plan. It's extremely rare to fly at both ends of a season. I hadn't laid any cards on the table; my season was about to begin.

We chose Boulder, on the slopes of the Rocky Mountains, to make our home away from home that year. I'd loved Boulder when I stayed there early in my career and was keen to head back before my days as a professional triathlete were up. It's the hometown of old triathlon friends Wes Hobson and Glynde Mangum, who helped with the arrangements. There are an endless supply of trails and quiet roads, and no shortage of people to train with. Greg Bennett and fellow Aussie Craig Alexander were in town with their wives, and Bevan was there too. It was a very social time, punctuated by lots of barbecues. Marisa particularly enjoyed my last two seasons because I was more relaxed after Athens. If I missed a few training sessions due to a muscle strain or the kids being sick, I didn't worry. At some psychological level I'd allowed myself to step back from the sport, and my performance prospered. In the two years after the Olympics my lowest placing was eighth.

I even got to spend time in Boulder with my old adversary Simon Lessing. He was born in South Africa, raised in England and now lives in the United States with his wife and two daughters. Our kids played together while we chatted about the Olympics. He was also disappointed in Sydney and left town straight after the race. When the British federation wanted him to jump through hoops to qualify for Athens, he walked away. He didn't see eye to eye with the ITU and so did very few World Cup races, but you can't argue with four world titles. In his day you couldn't get near him. He and Brad Beven were the two I couldn't beat early in my career, but because I won the Athens Olympics I feel as if I got the last laugh. Both Brad and Simon, who is still competitive in long-distance races, seem to be in it for the lifestyle these days, particularly Brad. If you haven't had the good fortune or the advisers to help you set up a life beyond the sport, you can get trapped and carry on training for lack of an alternative — travelling, racing, staying with friends, picking up a bit of money here and there. It can be a rootless existence. I don't know if that's how Brad's life is. It's not for me to say, and maybe he loves it. But it was strange for me to see him at the level he's at now, when I remember him as a great champion. It made me feel grateful that, thanks to Roger and Marisa, I was in a position to step out when I felt the time was right.

I was in good shape when I left Boulder — too good as it turned out. I won a World Cup race in Edmonton, then six days later pulled out one of my best-ever performances for third in the lucrative Lifetime Fitness race, once again on a flat course that didn't suit me, on a baking-hot day. For the second time in my career I ran myself into unconsciousness. I came around to a bleary whiteness. I was totally disorientated, but I was sure of one thing: I had no pants on. I figured something was up, because the bike pants I race in are bloody tight and take some getting off. Even more disconcerting was my next realisation — there was something stuck up my backside. Whoa! I had obviously been abducted by aliens who, determined to discover what made these strange triathlete creatures tick, were probing me. I was in a tent, packed in ice, an IV tube was dispatching clear droplets into my vein and my temperature was being monitored via a rectal thermometer. In a perverse way, I was chuffed. At the advanced age of 35, I thought I'd lost the ability to push myself that hard. Only Kemper, who slipped away on the bike, and renowned hot-weather specialist Volodymyr Polikarpenko had beaten me.

Pilone wasn't going to be happy. He hadn't wanted me to do two races so close together, but I'd promised to cruise at Edmonton. I did, and still won. Alongside Sydney in 1997, it was my easiest World Cup victory. A week later, I absolutely nailed myself and got beaten. Go figure. I was in terrific form, but the world championships were still six long weeks away. Form isn't static; you're either coming on or going backwards. I was facing a losing battle. That wasn't the only problem. In Edmonton I hadn't felt the buzz of victory that I usually did. A World Cup victory is a real prize, one that many very talented triathletes never experience, yet I'd felt quite ho-hum. I knew why: the Olympics had spoiled me. Everything else pales in comparison. I now understood the predicament Whitfield faced after winning the first Olympic triathlon in Sydney. All future achievements are measured against that — by yourself as well as others. His Olympic title came early in his career; I was lucky that Athens came late in mine. The scary question was how long I could find the motivation to stay at the top if the thrill of winning was fading. When someone knocks ever louder on your door, eventually you have to answer it.

Form and motivation, those were the question marks hanging over me as I flew to Europe to prepare for my 15th world championships. I made a spur-of-the-moment decision to race the London triathlon and had a shocker. I'd figured that if I was going to be training hard, I might as well race and do it chasing some money. I finished eighth, my lowest placing since the Olympics. There's something about that water in the Docklands: I can't swim in it. I'd also had a poor swim two years earlier when I used the race as a shakedown for Athens. The result did nothing for my morale. As far as form went, I thought I was on a one-way path to destruction. I was kicking myself, too, because making the call to do that race had meant leaving the United States and my family several days earlier than planned — and for what? The chance to humiliate myself at the world champs? Marisa and the kids had already flown home to Auckland and I wouldn't see them again for more than a month.

From London I went to Font-Romeu, a village in the Alps used as an altitude training base by French athletes. I had the company of a bunch of Kiwis — Gemmell, Warriner, Tanner — but I wasn't a happy camper. The small, basic rooms reminded me of my first time in Europe back in 1993 at Alpe d'Huez with Brett Sutton and the Aussies. Of course, the way I felt had nothing to do with the size of the rooms. I was homesick, struggling for motivation and wondering how to justify spending all this time half a world away from my family. I talked to Chris and we came up with a patch-up plan to try and extend my form across the gap to the worlds by doing high-mileage training at fairly low intensity. For the next 10 days I trained all day long, logging 170 km running and 500 km cycling, all at 2000 metres above sea level. It kept me fantastically fit, but mentally I didn't want to be there. One day I snapped and decided to go home. Marisa and Roger were horrified. 'Don't you dare,' they said. 'That's no way to finish your career.' Gemmell tried to encourage me too, telling me that I had to race the worlds because it was what I did and who I was. I reluctantly agreed to continue on to Belves in the south of France where the New Zealand team for the world championships was gathering for the last two weeks of preparation.

My key training session was to be done eight days before race day. Clark Ellice and Terrenzo Bozzone, two of the younger guys, were doing it with me. The workout was similar to the one I did in Pau that brought me to the boil for the Olympics: a two-hour hilly bike, immediately followed by running eight repetitions of 1000 m on an undulating stretch of road, with a minute of recovery between each lap. I was aiming to do each of them at between 2 min 55 sec and 3 min 05 sec. When we got to the last three I emphasised to the others the importance of keeping the quality up. On the sixth repetition, Terrenzo dropped me. Holy shit! It wasn't as though I was running poorly; he was flying. Be cool, I told myself, as we recovered before the seventh repetition. And then he did it again. Bloody little shit! However, this time I was sure that he'd pay for it on the last one. But he drilled it and dropped me again. It's an unwritten rule to never give your rivals a break, but I couldn't help telling him that if he raced like that he'd be the world champion.

I did my best not to let them see it, but I was gutted. To my mind, the caning that Terrenzo had dished out to me was confirmation that my time was up. I was convinced that I was going to get flogged at the worlds and that was an unbearable prospect; I wanted so much to race well. I emailed Pilone about what had happened and he asked what my times were. They were all in the target zone. He told me to forget about everyone else; I was in the right shape to have a great race. I heard what he said, but hearing and believing aren't the same thing. I got up and went to the pool as usual next morning, but I was like a zombie. I quit the session halfway through and emailed Roger that I was changing my tickets and coming home. I'd be seeing him soon in Auckland. That's when it was Rog to the rescue. He told me he was flying over to meet me at Lausanne airport and that I'd better be there. If he was prepared to drop everything and leave his wife and son for a week, well, I didn't have much choice. I learned later that he and Chris had got their heads together; Pilone had told Roger that I was fit but had lost the plot.

Rog was at the airport when the team arrived. Boy, was I glad to see him. The hassle of staying in the team hotel was the last thing I needed, so Rog smoothed the way with management. We'd attend the necessary meetings, he told them, but otherwise would do our own thing. They gave Roger a list of meeting times and on the way out of the airport, Rog dropped it in a rubbish bin. We drove out of Lausanne in our rental car and booked into a beautiful boutique hotel in the countryside. It was the beginning of a wonderful few days. It was like being on holiday in Europe with your best mate. We dined in lovely restaurants, took a boat trip on Lake Geneva, and had coffee in quaint villages. We could have been mistaken for a gay couple on a romantic trip away. I went for easy rides on peaceful rural lanes and just about forgot that in a few days' time I'd race for the title of world champion. When we dropped in to the team hotel to pick up my uniform, it was just as I'd expected. There were even schedules stuck on the wall. Bevan told me they were in bunkrooms, like a boarding hostel, with no television and nothing to do but stew about the race and listen to the trains rumbling by.

Two days before the race I rode over the hilly bike route and thought, 'Game on!' It was my sort of course. The race was still so far removed from my thoughts that I forgot until that night that I hadn't checked out the run. Roger and I drove into town after dinner and had a look. I felt detached, as though I didn't have a race to do at all. We stayed at our country hotel the night before too, and I arrived at the start feeling relaxed and ready.

It was a cracker race. I felt brilliant during the bike leg, where I was one of eight who rode away. 'Bloody Pilone, the tin-arse has done it again,' I thought. What struck me about the breakaway group was who wasn't there: no Aussies and, as I'd predicted, none of the Commonwealth Games medallists. Early in the run I found myself in the lead along with England's Tim Don. He'd finished more than three minutes behind me at the Olympics but had ridden well today and I knew that he could run. Halfway through, I lifted the pace to see how he responded. We were clipping over the ground, and although I felt good, I didn't feel the absolute magic I had in Athens or two months before at the Lifetime Fitness race in Minneapolis.

Don's not a great rider and I hoped the bike would have tired him more than me. We ran on, stride for stride. I reminded myself that I was in a dogfight and needed to stay focused. With 3 km to go, I pushed it up a gear but Don came with me and then took it to a new level. He didn't just accelerate over the top of me, he ran away. I pushed and pushed because there was always a chance he'd falter, but by the 1 km mark I'd launched everything I had. He was on fire. The margin between us at the finish was 17 seconds.

I was gutted to have come so close to the one title I'd chased for years that still eluded me, but proud to have raced so well. I'd flown the flag as Olympic champion and shown that if you wanted to win, first you had to get Carter. Considering that my form had peaked two months earlier and just a week before I'd had one foot on the plane home, it felt as if I'd burgled the result. People were slapping me on the back and pumping my hand. I caught sight of Rog among the crowd, straining to see me over a barrier. 'Good one, awesome,' he called. I yelled for him to climb over and join me. He waved me away. 'No, no, I'm okay.' It was a classic Roger and Hamish moment. Here was I, getting the plaudits, and there was Rog, the guy who'd dropped everything to fly around the world to save me from myself, elbowed aside again.

I walked away thinking it was a job well done. I had no idea that would be my last World Cup triathlon.

NO REGRETS

One month after the world championships, I heard that Tim Don had missed a doping test. I didn't think much of it; anyone might miss one. But then I heard that he'd missed three — all before the race in Lausanne. The first test, I was told, was before the 2005 World Championships, the second before the Commonwealth Games, and the third in the middle of the 2006 season. If that was the case, Don shouldn't have been on the start line at the world championships. What transpired in his case was farcical and damaging to the sport of triathlon. The British Triathlon Association kept quiet about the missed tests until after the world championships, then announced a three-month ban near the end of the season, when Don was off on holiday. It wasn't a ban at all; it was a joke.

Discussing this is difficult for me because some people will wrongly assume that my view is coloured by finishing second to Tim and won't give any thought to the wider issues involved. What happened is much bigger than Tim or me. Combating doping is a serious problem; it has ruined many sports and I'd hate that to happen to triathlon. I wouldn't want to take the win at Lausanne through disqualification. We raced and he beat me. I don't know Don well, but I assume he's clean. The point is that we all live by the same rules: if you miss three tests within an 18-month period, then you're banned. The ban should start when the third test is missed and not when it suits the athlete or his federation. Don attributed his missed tests to forgetfulness and the complexity of a process requiring athletes to update an online database with their whereabouts. Whether the system was difficult to use is also irrelevant. He wasn't the only one who had to use it. I have never missed a drug test in my whole career. Had I missed two drug tests — knowing the boom would drop if I missed another through error or oversight — I would have been on the phone to the head of the anti-doping agency making sure that they had my cellphone number and knew exactly where I was each day. We are professional athletes and should be able to conduct all facets of the business in a professional way.

Just as disappointing was the failure of the International Triathlon Union to act. ITU chairman Les McDonald didn't seem interested. When I asked what he proposed to do, McDonald told me that the ITU couldn't control the actions of a national federation. That may be so, but the ITU, as the sport's world body, sets the tone (by action or omission) as to what is acceptable. There was nothing to stop the ITU coming out with a clear public statement. Had Les said that it was unacceptable for someone who had missed three tests to be able to line up at the world championships because the athlete's federation had delayed action, it would at least have been a stake in the ground. I'd have been happy with that. Instead the ITU shrugged its shoulders. McDonald didn't inspire confidence.

I was on the verge of retiring after Lausanne. My lack of elation at winning the Edmonton World Cup race and my flagging enthusiasm before the worlds were telling signs. But stepping out isn't simple if there's nothing else to step into, so I decided I'd continue to race in 2007, although I had already ruled out the Beijing Olympics in my own mind. I decided to do the Xterra World Championship race in Hawaii in late October. There was US$25,000 on the line and, as it's more relaxed than the triathlon world championships, Marisa and I left the kids with family and treated it as a bit of a holiday. Xterra is a rugged, cross-country version of triathlon. This race comprised a 1.5 km sea swim, 40 km mountain-bike and 10 km run — the latter legs over rough lava trails, rocks and sand. There's not the same depth of competition, but the event is bloody hard. My time was 2 hr 42 min, about an hour longer than I'm used to racing. Riding the bike course before the race was an eye-opener. One terrifying section was a sea of loose rocks that was barely rideable. In fact I had to dismount, as it happened, at the exact moment a group of Xterra specialists rode past. One called out that I wouldn't be able to walk in the race if I wanted to be in the hunt.

On the day itself, I found myself in the lead with Olivier Marceau early on in the ride. I didn't see any of the guys who'd ridden past me when I was scouting the course, so I guess that was sweet revenge. It was fitting to have Olivier with me in what turned out to be my last race as a professional athlete. I don't know how many times we've been in the lead together during the bike, but you'd need your toes as well as your fingers to count them. He put in his usual strong ride and when my back tyre began to hiss with escaping air it looked good for him. I nursed the bike for the last few kilometres and started the run 1 min 20 sec behind. The terrain was so hard that I felt like I was grovelling, but I caught Olivier and won by 19 seconds. It turned out to be a nice end to my career: I'd won my only world title in my last race.

Since Athens, I'd tried to create more interesting challenges for myself by doing fewer World Cups, which I'd raced my entire career, and adding into my schedule more of those with a different format, such as Xterra, Escape from Alcatraz, Lifetime Fitness and the Chicago triathlon. I felt I'd done it all, except long-distance triathlons, which didn't appeal. One more year would give me time to plan what came after retirement and I could chase some good-money races. We could all go back to Boulder and have a great family holiday. It'd be just like a cricketer's testimonial year. However, it's never a good sign when you're not racing for the joy of it and the pure desire to win. Money isn't powerful enough to motivate you through a bad patch in a race.

Soon after Christmas, as I was planning my 2007 season, a bomb landed in my lap. I was introduced to Rod Drury and his business partner, Hamish Edwards. Over lunch they explained who they were, what they were planning and where I could fit into those plans. Rod is an information technology (IT) specialist who's won New Zealand Entrepreneur of the Year, and his new product, Xero, is an online accounting package for small to medium businesses. I liked him and could see how I could help with client relationships, but I knew nothing about accounting. Rod told me that my background was ideal because I'd been successful in a small business — the business of Hamish Carter, athlete. It was a start-up venture, which is always risky, but I was excited by the prospect of that sort of challenge. Rod was willing to allow me time to fulfil my sponsorship commitments, with my role at Xero increasing as time passed. It seemed exactly what I'd been looking for.

I had to make my mind up once and for all: was I ready to retire? I was approaching my 36th birthday, but was racing as well as ever. Pilone put it in a nutshell: did I want to go to Beijing? My answer was an emphatic 'No'. 'Well,' he said, 'why the hell are you racing?' Aside from the hard work and long months away from family, you need a desperate hunger to race well at the Olympics. I couldn't see myself standing on the pontoon at the start in Beijing a better athlete than I was at Athens. I would have loved to have held the title of world champion, too, but when it comes down to it, how much would that really have added to my life? I was done; it was time to go and, most importantly, I felt I could go with no regrets. Doing my best to help build a global tech company will be my next Olympics. Bloody hell, I was about to begin the first 'normal' job of my life. I announced my retirement on television on 6 March 2007. I wanted to tell friends personally, but there were too many to ring, so I emailed them this message:

> *'Dear fellow athletes,*
>
> *Just wanted to drop you a short note to let you know I am retiring from triathlon today. The time has come. I have enjoyed the past 14 years racing you all, sometimes beating you but mostly getting beaten! The friendships you make in our sport are incredible and I will remember*

these and the fun times I've had longer than any results.

Those that I have caused to crash or have smashed in training or drowned going around a mark I am truly ***not*** *sorry! As athletes in a bloody tough sport we all take a beating more often than not. I wouldn't trade this for the world. So good luck and race hard. I will toast you every step of the way with a gin and tonic.*

Never give up.

Hamish'

I leave with New Zealand's ranks in pretty good shape. In Andrea Hewitt, Debbie Tanner and Sam Warriner, we finally have three truly world-class athletes and there are some talented women close behind them. Among the men, there's an opportunity for someone else to step up. Bevan Docherty and Kris Gemmell are clearly on top, but then there's a big gap. Kris had his best result with a fourth at the worlds in Lausanne, but it was a long way back to the other Kiwis, Shane Reed and Terrenzo Bozzone in 40th and 41st respectively — more than six minutes off the pace. Terrenzo has all the talent in the world, as he showed when he whipped me in that key training session before the world championships, but talent is only one part of the package and not necessarily the most important. He's capable of getting to the top in the open ranks. He's young and still learning, but I worry for him. Being a champion junior can be a curse because you get lumbered with big expectations. I hope he makes it, but he's got a way to go and some very tough guys to beat on the way.

Bevan didn't finish in Lausanne and nor did Brad Kahlefeldt, the Australian who beat him for the gold at the Commonwealth Games at the start of the season. The other Games medallist, Peter Robertson, backed up well for sixth. It's not impossible, but it is damn hard to be flying at both of the season's two big events when they are so far apart.

Bevan Docherty

Hamish knows what it takes to get to a world-winning level and he's very good at peaking for those days. That's his key. He's focused and he's selfish. To be one of the best, you need to be both those things, and he's very lucky to have Marisa who understands and allows him to really concentrate on his training.

Running down the finishing straight at Athens, I could see Hamish just ahead, but I wasn't thinking that I'd lost gold, I was thinking I'd won silver. There was no disappointment that day whatsoever. It hurts now, to be second, but being part of a Kiwi one-two is very special. I went out on a bike ride with him soon after he announced his retirement and I was quizzing him, saying, 'Hang on, are you sure you're retiring?' My biggest regret is getting sick with a blood infection and fever at the Lausanne World Championships. We were both in great shape and not being able to have one last rematch will probably haunt me for the rest of my life.

I guess I will be remembered for that race in Athens and that's fine by me. I'll never forget it either, and nor will I forget Sydney, because to me they were absolutely linked. Without Sydney, I'm sure Athens wouldn't have happened; my success was sown in my failures. I've competed in more than 100 races, with a win-loss ratio of about one in four and I was lucky that one of those wins was in a race where the whole world took notice. In 2000 I had some growing to do. Having a family brought balance and, finally, I came to understand the first part of that old rowing mantra, 'timing and balance'. Through it all, I learnt that timing and balance is the key to success. That's not to downplay plain bloody hard work — that's a given for anything worthwhile — but to capitalise on that hard work, you have to be smart and strategic: a thinking athlete. Timing gives you balance and balance gives you timing. Those two pillars, along with the pain and grind of hard work, give you the confidence and clarity to be great.

I'm proud that I was able to build a team around me that helped achieve success. There isn't a lot of money in triathlon, but with Roger I was able to turn it into a successful business. Results were important, of course, but so was how we conducted ourselves. Money didn't just pour in after Athens. It isn't like winning a major in golf or tennis, where you wake up and there's a million dollars in your bank account. For me, each relationship with a sponsor is an ongoing commitment. It's more than a job because it's the people and companies that had the faith and vision to want me to help build their brand while I chased what began as a schoolboy's dream. Their support helped make my success possible. It's enormously satisfying to know that our house is paid for primarily from doing something that I loved. How important is a dream? It's what life is all about. It gives you your life force every day when you wake. Some won't chase a dream for fear they'll fail, but failure is often the very pathway to achieving that dream. Had I been beaten in Athens, I still would have been glad that I'd striven for my goal and didn't quit, because that is success in itself.

I'm amazed how that race caught people's imaginations. Three years on, I'm still asked to speak about it. If what I did inspires a few kids, as John Walker inspired me, well, that really is more than I ever dreamed. It took a couple of years to get around to it, but we've hung a photo of me finishing in Athens on the wall at home. The medal is in an Oakley sunglasses bag, in a pot where we keep the spare keys. I rarely look at it. Don't need to; I know it's there.

Career Highlights

1993
World Championships, Manchester, 3rd
World Cup, Hawaii, 1st

1994
World Cup, Sion, Switzerland, 1st

1995
World Cup, Auckland, 1st
World ranking: 2

1996
World Championships, 9th

1997
World Cup, Cancun, Mexico, 1st
World Cup, Sydney, Australia, 1st
World Championships, 2nd
World ranking: 2

1998
World Cup, Auckland, 1st
World Cup, Tiszaujvaros, Hungary, 1st
World Championships: 4th
World ranking: 1

1999
World Cup, Tiszaujvaros, Hungary, 1st
Oceania Championships, 2nd
World ranking: 1

2000

World Cup, Hawaii, 1st
World Championships, 5th
World ranking: 1

2001

Goodwill Games, 2nd
World ranking: 4

2002

Oceania Championships, 1st
Commonwealth Games, 3rd
World ranking: 1

2003

World Cup, Corner Brook, Canada, 1st
World Championships, 5th
Oceania Championships, 1st

2004

Olympic Games, 1st
World Championships, 6th
New Zealand Sportsman of the Year

2005

Chicago Triathlon, 1st
Escape from Alcatraz, 2nd
World Championships, 4th

2006

World Cup, Edmonton, Canada, 1st
World Championships, 2nd
Xterra World Championships, 1st